P9-CNB-250

DISCARD

POWERFUL
PHRASES
for
Successful Interviews

POWERFUL PHRASES

for

Successful Interviews

* * *

Over 400 Ready-to-Use Words and Phrases
That Will Get You the Job You Want

Tony Beshara

FOREWORD BY

Dr. Phil McGraw

AMACOM

AMERICAN MANAGEMENT ASSOCIATION

New York • Atlanta • Brussels • Chicago • Mexico City • San Francisco
Shanghai • Tokyo • Toronto • Washington, D.C.

Bulk discounts available. For details visit:
www.amacombooks.org/go/specialsales
Or contact special sales:
Phone: 800-250-5308
E-mail: specialsls@amanet.org
View all the AMACOM titles at: www.amacombooks.org
American Management Association: www.amanet.org

This publication is designed to provide accurate and authoritative information in regard to the subject matter covered. It is sold with the understanding that the publisher is not engaged in rendering legal, accounting, or other professional service. If legal advice or other expert assistance is required, the services of a competent professional person should be sought.

Library of Congress Cataloging-in-Publication Data

Beshara, Tony, 1948–
Power phrases for successful interviews : over 400 ready-to-use words and phrases that will get you the job you want / Tony Beshara ; foreword by Dr. Phil McGraw.—1 Edition.
pages cm
Includes bibliographical references and index.
ISBN-13: 978-0-8144-3354-6 (alk. paper)
ISBN-10: 0-8144-3354-5 (alk. paper)
1. Employment interviewing.   2. Job hunting.   3. English language—Terms and phrases.   I. Title.
HF5549.5.I6B47157 2014
650.14'4—dc23   2013042989

© 2014 Tony Beshara.

All rights reserved.

Printed in the United States of America.

This publication may not be reproduced, stored in a retrieval system, or transmitted in whole or in part, in any form or by any means, electronic, mechanical, photocopying, recording, or otherwise, without the prior written permission of AMACOM, a division of American Management Association, 1601 Broadway, New York, NY 10019.

The scanning, uploading, or distribution of this book via the Internet or any other means without the express permission of the publisher is illegal and punishable by law. Please purchase only authorized electronic editions of this work and do not participate in or encourage piracy of copyrighted materials, electronically or otherwise. Your support of the author's rights is appreciated.

About AMA

American Management Association (www.amanet.org) is a world leader in talent development, advancing the skills of individuals to drive business success. Our mission is to support the goals of individuals and organizations through a complete range of products and services, including classroom and virtual seminars, webcasts, webinars, podcasts, conferences, corporate and government solutions, business books, and research. AMA's approach to improving performance combines experiential learning—learning through doing—with opportunities for ongoing professional growth at every step of one's career journey.

Printing number

ACC LIBRARY SERVICES AUSTIN, TX

*As always, dedicated to God's greatest blessings,
my wonderful wife and best friend, Chrissy, and our wonderful family.*

CONTENTS

FOREWORD
by Dr. Phil

We all know it is tough out there with so much competition for every job worth having. What you need is an "edge"—the inside information on what interviewers really want to hear and clear instruction on how to deliver it. That edge is Tony Beshara, and he has put everything you need to stand out in the crowd right here in this book.

Interviewers' questions can be challenging, and knowing the right words to say at interviews doesn't come naturally. We've all been in interviews where we've said the wrong thing, which can make the difference in getting hired or not. On the other hand, saying the right thing in just the right way can turn a ho-hum interview into a home run.

Tony Beshara knows the ropes like no one you have ever encountered. Tony has personally helped close to 10,000 people find jobs, because he knows exactly what employers are looking for, including the key words and phrases that will get people follow-up interviews and job offers.

In this book he has distilled his decades of wisdom and experience into more than 400 easy-to-apply words and phrases. Whether you're entry level or an executive, consult this book and you'll be confidently prepared for every interviewing situation, from nailing down the initial interview to negotiating your job offer.

I have seen it happen firsthand. Over the years on the *Dr. Phil* show I've depended on Tony Beshara countless times to find jobs for badly discouraged guests. Tony is the very best there is at preparing candidates and then getting them jobs. Adopt his thinking, and in my opinion you will have an incredible advantage.

ACKNOWLEDGMENTS

As always, the greatest thanks go to Chrissy for her prayers, time, and spiritual support. The AMACOM team was wonderful as always: Ellen, Barry, Jim, and Kama, thank you so much! And, again, a special thanks to the thousands of candidates and hiring authorities I have worked with over the years who have contributed to this book's contents.

POWERFUL PHRASES

for

Successful Interviews

INTRODUCTION
Why Powerful Phrases Make a Difference

Interviewing, finding a job, and hiring are considered among the most important business endeavors, so it might surprise you to know that the average professional hire in America involves only four hours of face-to-face interviewing. Though the emotional intensity for both finding a job and hiring are great, a job seeker should be aware that the time to make a successful impression on interviewing and hiring authorities is very short. In fact, hiring decisions are made more quickly than business managers and leaders like to admit. One McGill University study showed that most interviewers make up their mind to hire someone in the first four minutes of the interview!

Psychologists have proven, and my own experience confirms, that in the interviewing process, employers evaluate job candidates on the basis of a few—very few—real facts, and 90 percent of the hiring decision is made emotionally. Candidates are hired because of a few little things they do or say, and the rest is emotional justification. Psychologists call this "motivated reasoning." A

1

plethora of recent business and psychology books and articles by authors like Jonah Lehrer and Leonard Mlodinow demonstrates that most business decisions are made subliminally, with more emotion than logic. While the majority of job candidates are trying to be "competent" in the interviewing process, the successful ones focus on being liked and remembered. They use powerful words and phrases to accomplish this.

You are going to be judged quickly and emotionally as a job candidate, so if you say the right things by using the right words, you stand out and are more likely to get hired. So little real face-to-face time is spent interviewing that hiring authorities make their decisions based on a few memorable phrases (good or bad) that a candidate uses.

Use the right phrases, and you are remembered and thought of highly; you are more likely to get hired. Use the wrong phrases, and you are forgotten when you walk out of the room; you are certain to lose the job opportunity.

THE SUCCESSFUL APPLICATION OF POWERFUL PHRASES

I'll give you a perfect example of just what I mean about how powerful phrases can make a difference. You will learn in Chapter 3 that I recommend two very powerful phrases to be used at the end of the first interview:

1. *"How do I stack up with the other candidates you have interviewed?"*
2. *"What do I need to do to get the job?"*

Recently, one of our clients interviewed seven candidates. The only candidate that we referred used these two phrases to close the initial interview. The hiring authority remarked to the candidate—and later to us—that she was the only one of the seven candidates who actually asked how she compared to the others.

In fact, as the hiring authority passed the candidate to the second group of interviewing authorities, he told his associates, "I interviewed seven candidates and this lady was the only one who asked for the job. I really like her." The candidate, by the way, used the same power phrases, as well as others you will learn in Chapter 7, for her follow-up interviews to land the job.

This was a mid-level purchasing manager position. The candidate only spent a total of two-and-a-half hours interviewing at the company: one hour at the initial interview and an hour-and-a-half with others in the company. The hiring and interviewing authorities did spend more time checking previous employment references and so on, but the candidate acknowledged that she became the "best" candidate because of the power phrases she used in the interviewing process.

These two powerful phrases made all the difference in the world. The vice president of procurement openly admitted that our candidate was not the most qualified applicant. But, he said she interviewed better than the others. Even the candidate herself admitted that she didn't seem to interview especially well except for her closing phrases. She is absolutely convinced that those two small phrases won her the job.

Powerful Phrases for Successful Interviews is filled with similar phrases that will enable you to raise yourself to the top of the candidate pool, whatever the job, whatever the company, and whoever is doing the hiring. It is meant to be a quick reference to specific words and phrases to use at every stage of a successful job search. You will learn the most effective, short, simple, and expert phrases to gain an advantage in getting interviews, performing well on initial and follow-up interviews, handling the toughest questions to dispel any lingering doubt on the part of the hiring authority, and negotiating a strong job offer. You will have the right words to make the difference every time.

Powerful Phrases to Get Face-to-Face Interviews

The most important thing you can do to get a job is to interview. Nothing else matters unless you can get a face-to-face interview with a hiring manager—someone with authority (to hire) and pain (an urgent need to hire). Learning to use the right words and phrases can make getting an interview easier.

Most people are uncomfortable with selling other people on interviewing them with the possibility of being hired. It can be daunting, burdensome, and an excruciating task. No one likes to be rejected. And there are fewer more clear-cut rejections than being denied an interview or being rejected for a job.

The risk of being rejected goes with the process of getting interviews and being interviewed. The sooner you face that reality and prepare for this kind of rejection, the sooner you're going to be able to find a job. Pristine résumés, brilliant research, great contacts, even superior previous job performance, will not help you find a job anywhere near the extent that getting numerous interviews and performing well in each interview will.

The initial interviews, if they're successful, will lead to subsequent second, third, or fourth interviews that will eventually land you a job. The most effective thing you can do is to pick up the phone and call anyone and everyone you can, whether you know them or not, to find people who might be able to grant you time for an interview.

CONTACTING PEOPLE YOU KNOW

The easiest place to start looking to set up interviews is with people you know. Here are the first people you want to contact and ask for the opportunity to interview:

→ Previous employers, peers, and subordinates
→ Family
→ Friends
→ Acquaintances
→ Competitors
→ Suppliers and distributors
→ Customers

Note that it is important for you to record the telephone number and date you call people. You may be calling the person back again in thirty, sixty, or ninety days. Many people will not respond to you positively for a month or two. You want to remind them that you need a job!

Let's start with words and phrases to use in contacting people you know. Keep these in front of you as you make the call!

Previous *Employers*, Peers, Subordinates, Friends, and Acquaintances

No matter how well you know the person, start your call with a simple introduction:

> *Hello, _____ this is_____ (your name). We know each other from _____.*

This prepares the way for the phrase stating the reason for your call:

> *I am currently looking for a new job. I called to ask if you know of any job opportunities available either with your firm or any others you might know about.*

Then provide a quick update on your job situation:

> *For the past_____ (time period), I have been working at _____ (company). I am looking for a job as _____. Can you think of anyone who might need what I can offer?*

(Very long pause) . . . If the answer is no, then say:

> *I really appreciate your time. I'd like to send you my résumé, and if you can think of anyone who might be interested, please pass it along to them.*
>
> *I am not sure how long my search will take. I'd like to call you back in a month or so to see if you might have thought of anyone who might be interested. Would that be all right?*

This way, you've laid the groundwork for further contact down the road. And sending your résumé will provide a tangible reminder of your ongoing job search. (Very few people will tell you not to send your résumé.)

Family

With family members, your approach is basically the same:

> *Hello,* _____. *This is* _____ (your cousin, brother-in-law, or other relation). *I called to ask you if you know of any job opportunities that might be available. For the past* _____(time period), *I have been working at* _____(name of company or what you have been doing). *I am presently looking for a job. Can you think of anyone that might need what I can offer?*

(Long pause) . . . If the person says no, then say:

> *I really appreciate your time. I'd like to send you my ré-sumé and if you can think of anyone who might be interested, please pass it along to them.*
>
> *I am not sure how long my search will take; I'd like to call you back in a month or so to see if you might have thought of anyone that might be interested. Would that be all right?*

Again, it's unlikely that relatives will say no to receiving a résumé, even if they don't think they can be of help.

Competitors, Suppliers, and Customers

Here you're approaching people you know through business. Start with a quick reminder of who you are and how you know them.

> *Hello,_____. This is _____. We know each other from being a _____* (competitors, customers, or suppliers). *I called you to ask if you know of any job opportunities that might be available. Most recently I have been _____* (describe what you have been doing). *I am presently looking for a job. Would your organization be in need of a good _____?*

(Long pause) . . . If the person says no, then say:

> *I really appreciate your time. I'd like to send you my résumé and if you can think of anyone who might be interested, please pass it along to them.*
>
> *By the way, I am not sure how long my search will take; I'd like to call you back in a month or so to see if you have thought of anyone that might be interested. Would that be all right?*

Once again, you finish by asking if it would be all right for you to send your résumé and call back in a month or so to see if the person has thought of anyone who might be interested.

CALLING PEOPLE YOU *DON'T* KNOW

This part of the process can make a big difference in how fast you find a new job. The procedure is simple: You get on the telephone and present yourself to a prospective employer and ask for an interview. This is known as a cold call. It is simple and direct. The results you get will be immediate. The cold call will either result in an interview or it won't.

The process of doing this is very simple, but the manner in which you do it is sophisticated and takes a lot of courage and practice. The reason it takes courage is because you are running the risk of being rejected within ten seconds. On top of that, you probably are going to have to make about 75 to 100 of these calls before you get an interview. So, you have to expect plenty of rejection before you get positive reinforcement.

Keep in mind that when you do this, you are trying to get an interview regardless of whether or not there is a position open. You are selling an interview, not necessarily selling the idea of getting a job. It is extremely important that you recognize this difference. The purpose of this call is to get in front of a prospective employer so you can sell yourself and your skills. You are purposely going to ask for a meeting with the prospective employer without asking if there indeed is a need. Don't confuse getting hired with getting an initial interview. All you're trying to do is sell an audience with that person.

The reason that you are just trying to sell the initial audience, or interview, is that, very often, hiring managers will interview potential employees whether they have an opening or not. As you will see, the phrases to use do not ask if there are any openings; they ask for an appointment, an interview, and do not presume a current or upcoming position opening.

Whom to Call

If you don't know the name of a hiring manager within a firm when you call an organization, simply ask the name of the manager of the department that you would normally report to. If you are an accountant, call and ask for the name of the controller. If you are a controller, call and ask for the name of the vice president of finance or the chief financial officer (CFO) or, when it comes down to it, anyone who is in charge of the finances for the company. If you are a salesperson, you should call and ask for the sales manager, the regional sales manager, the vice president of sales, and so forth. If you are an administrative support person, then you would ask for the administrative support manager. When you call, ask for the manager of the kind of department that your skills and ability would fit. It is that simple.

In larger organizations, the people who are answering the phone are instructed to *not* give out that kind of information. They may tell you just that, or they will tell you that they don't know, or that they don't have the titles of the people in the company. So, you can do two or three easy things:

→ You can go online to the company's website and find the names of the people that are in charge.

→ You can ask for the customer service department or the person in charge of customer service. They will be quite helpful.

→ You can ask for the accounts payable department. These people are so used to getting beat up every day by vendors asking for money that when they speak to someone nice, who is just asking them for a name, they are usually so grateful, they will tell you anything, especially something so simple as who the managers are.

Now, if you get "lost" in the voice mail system that only allows you to spell the names of people, you are going to get very frustrated. If you know the name of the person you're trying to reach, of course, spell their name. Some companies' voice mail systems purposely *don't* include the names of some of the managers. (I know it's stupid, and it makes absolutely no sense, but I don't write the rules.)

If you run into this, your goal is to speak to just about anybody. So hit the first letter of any common name like "S" and speak to whoever answers. Ask for the accounting department, sales department, customer service department, and so on. If you don't know the name of the manager of the department you need to speak with and you get a voice mail from one of the administrative people, you have no choice but to leave a message and ask them to call you back. I would not recommend telling them why you are calling. When they call back, be as nice and cordial as you can. You want to speak to their department manager. Most of the time, administrative types want to help, so they will give you the name of the manager. Try to speak to the manager right then.

If you have skills that can transfer from one industry or profession to another you can cold call just about anybody. For example, any kind of administrative, accounting, bookkeeping, or sales experience can carry over to a lot of different businesses. So, you can cold call from just about any reference book that might provide names of companies and telephone numbers. Don't overlook the white pages of businesses or the online telephone book itself.

What to Say

You want to get past the initial responder as quickly as possible, so you should start with a direct question:

Hello, who is your _____ (controller, vice president of sales, information technology (IT) director, CEO, or other title)? *Fine, let me speak with* _____ _____.

If you are put through to the person you wish to speak with, get right to the point by stating who you are and what you want:

Hello, _____, my name is _____, and I am with _____ and have a great track record of _____. I would like to meet with you to discuss my potential with your firm. Would tomorrow morning at 9 AM be good for you or would tomorrow afternoon at 3 PM be better?

If you get a response like, "I really don't have any openings," then your response should be:

I understand and the kind of person that I want to work for probably does not presently have an opening.

I would just like to take fifteen or twenty minutes of your time because I am a top-notch performer. I am the kind of person whom you would want to know to either replace your weakest link or to be aware of my availability when the next opening does occur. Now, would tomorrow morning be good for you or is tomorrow afternoon better?

You will either get the appointment or a more insistent response of, "I really don't have any openings. There is no reason for us to meet."

At this point, you have nothing to lose, so you might as well state your case as strongly as you can:

I understand that you don't have any immediate openings, but I have a great track record of_____ _____.

I am the kind of professional who is better than 90 percent of the employees you might have now.

It is to you and your company's best interest that you at least talk to me and be aware of my availability. If not for now, then maybe in the future. My experience has taught me that, often, great talent comes along when you don't need it. But, it is always a good idea to be aware of talent on a face-to-face basis.

I will only take a few moments of your time and it may wind up being beneficial for all of us. Would tomorrow morning or tomorrow afternoon be better?

If the response is, "Can you e-mail me a résumé?" your answer is:

I can, but my résumé is only one-dimensional and it is of value for both of us to associate a face and a personality with a résumé. I'd like to bring it by, hand deliver it to you, and spend maybe fifteen minutes of your time so that you know what my accomplishments are and how they can benefit you and your company. Is tomorrow morning good or would tomorrow afternoon be better?

If the response is an emphatic, "Please just e-mail me the résumé!" (just a nice way of saying no), then your response is:

I'll do that right now. I will call you back tomorrow to be sure you have received it, and then we can set up a visit.

If you get a very emphatic no, and it is clear that you're not going to get any kind of face-to-face interview, you then need to pause for two or three seconds and say:

Do you know of any other opportunities that might exist in your firm with another manager?

If you get a person's name, ask:

May I use your name as a reference?

If you get the name of another manager, also ask for his or her phone number.

If the answer is "no" to your question about other opportunities with the company, then ask (after a two- or three-second pause):

Do you know of any other organization that you might have heard of through the grapevine that might need someone of my experience?

If you get the name of an organization or a person's name, again be sure to ask:

May I use your name as a reference?

Powerful Phrases for Referrals

If you get a referral to a particular person or organization and the person who referred you said you could use his or her name (this is an indication of how strong the ties are between them), here are the words and phrases to use:

Hello, Mr./Ms. _____. I was referred to you by _____. I am _____ with _____ and a great track record of _____.

I would like to meet with you to discuss my potential with your firm. Would tomorrow morning at 9 AM be good for you or would tomorrow afternoon at 3 PM be better?

You will be amazed at the number of job opportunities you will uncover this way.

Controllers know other controllers. Vice presidents of sales know other vice presidents of sales. Engineering managers know other engineering managers, and so on. It is not uncommon for one type of manager to know a number of other types of managers both within and outside of their own company. Their counterparts in other organizations often ask these managers if they indeed know somebody to fill vacant positions. You may only get a productive response one out of every forty times you try this approach. But don't be discouraged. The one interview you get as a result of asking that question is worth the forty or fifty times of asking.

Whether you get a referral or not, it is a very good idea to end the conversation with the following:

Thank you for your time, I would at least like to e-mail you my résumé in case something might change with you or someone you know.

Nine out of ten times, the person on the other end of the phone will be willing to receive the résumé. No matter what the person's response, whether it be positive or not, end the conversation by saying:

I'd like to give you a call back in thirty days or so to see if there might be any openings there or if you might know of any openings with friends of yours.

Again, nine out of ten people will agree to your doing that. To a certain extent, that lets people off the hook for the moment; but they also know, in the back of their minds, that they could easily have a position open up at any time.

Here's a key point: Cold calling is a numbers game. The more calls you make, the more likely you are to get an interview.

If the hiring manager just plain dismisses you or insists that you deal with the human resources (HR) department, you can say:

> *My experience with company HR departments, as far as identifying top talent when there isn't an immediate need, just hasn't been good. I am sure they are wonderful people; but I need to be talking to decisive managers who can make immediate decisions. Is there any other manager in your firm who has an opening?*

HOW TO MAKE COLD CALLING WORK

This is very simple but very strong stuff. The idea is to sell a face-to-face interview whether the hiring manager has a position opening or not. You are not asking if there is a job opening or asking to be hired; you're simply getting a face-to-face interview. The powerful phrases you use are meant to be forceful and to the point.

There are a few crucial aspects of this approach. First, do not ask the person answering the phone who does the hiring. You'll probably be relegated to the HR department and that for the most part is a dead end.

Once you get a hiring authority on the phone, you have to provide features, advantages, and benefits as to why you should be interviewed. This is very important! If you simply call and ask for an interview without giving specific reasons in the form of features, advantages, and benefits to the prospective employer, you won't get to first base. This is, again, simple stuff if you are aware of what you are doing.

Here's an example:

*Hello, Mr. or Ms._____. My name is_____.
I am a solid mechanical engineer (feature). I am registered with fifteen years of very stable engineering experience (feature). I have worked my way up in two organizations from the ground floor to a senior engineer position (feature). The <u>advantage</u> that I bring is stability and performance. The <u>benefit</u> to you and your organization is that you would have a long-term employee with a great track record.*

I would like to meet with you to discuss my potential with your firm. Would tomorrow morning at 10:00 AM or tomorrow afternoon at 2:00 PM be the best for you?

Another example would be:

Hello, Mr. or Ms._____. My name is_____ and I am an accomplished IT professional. I have ten solid years of experience, five with a Fortune 500 firm and five with a small $100 million distribution firm (features). I have attained nine IT certifications (advantage) as well as saved each one of the firms I have worked for thousands of IT dollars. I would like to (benefit) continue this kind of a performance with an organization like yours.

I would like to meet with you to discuss my potential with your firm. Would Tuesday morning at 9:00 AM or Wednesday afternoon at 3:00 PM work the best for you?

Your Own Statement of Features, Advantages, and Benefits

The purpose of this approach is to briefly and succinctly tell a hiring authority your personal features and advantages so that they can be perceived as benefits to the hiring authority's company. So, your job now is to come up with a statement of features, advantages, and benefits about yourself. The question is, and always will be, on the part of that hiring authority, "Why should I hire you?" The whole interviewing process centers on this question.

Features, advantages, and benefits regarding you and your possible employment do not have to be mystical, miraculous, or mesmerizing. They can be simple and rather uncomplicated. In fact, simple and uncomplicated reasons for hiring somebody are the best. So, the next exercise is to come up with a features, advantages, and benefits statement about you.

A *feature* is an aspect of you or your career that makes you unique. It can be the number of years of experience. It can be grades in school. It can be things like hard work, determination, persistence, and dedication. A feature, in a job-seeking situation, is simply a unique aspect about you that is going to be translated into being a good employee.

An *advantage* is something that the feature does to set you apart from the average. So, if you graduated cum laude from college and worked your way through college with two jobs (features), you have demonstrated hard work and commitment way above the average person (advantage).

A *benefit* would be the gain that a company would realize from hiring a person who brings unique features and advantages. So, the features of graduating at the top of your class as well as working two jobs demonstrated your advantage to perform on a higher level than average; therefore, you will perform in the same way for whoever you work for and the company will benefit from your work.

So now, write out your own:

Features: _____

Advantages: _____

Benefits: _____

Keeping in mind that you are selling yourself and that you are briefly giving a prospective employer a reason for why he ought to interview you, write a features, advantages, and benefits statement about yourself:

*Hello, Mr. or Ms.*_____*. My name is*
_____*. I am a* _____*. I* (features)_____*, which are* (advantages) _____*, and, therefore,* _____(benefits) *you and your firm.*

Practice writing this, and in just a few minutes you can write three or four features, advantages, and benefits statements on yourself to fit just about any situation. Remember, the purpose of this statement is to intrigue a hiring authority enough to want to interview you. Do not try to sell the whole idea of hiring you in one phone call. The purpose is to get the interview by giving a hiring authority a brief statement about what you can do for him or her.

Ending the Cold Call

The closing question to use in any cold-calling situation is:

Could I see you tomorrow morning or would tomorrow afternoon be better?

This presents the hiring authority with a minor choice resulting in a major decision, which most salespeople learn in their first training class. This concept is so simple, it is almost too good, and yet a phenomenal number of people will avoid using it because it appears so obviously manipulative.

It definitely is simple, but it also definitely works! At the end of your features, advantages, and benefits statement, ask the minor choice and major decision question. It works. Do not ask questions such as these: "Would you be interested in talking with me?" or "Could I come by and see you?" or "Can we set a date for an interview?" None of these questions are nearly as effective as:

Could I see you tomorrow morning at 9 AM or would tomorrow afternoon at 2 PM be better?"

Please don't try to be coy or cutesy by making this more complicated than it needs to be. Simply make the features, advantages, and benefits statement and ask the alternative choice question. Then, shut up! Don't say another word until you have a response.

Now, most people who are not in sales, and even some who are, will have a difficult time using this statement and question, especially in the beginning of their job search. I have been using this format for finding other people jobs since 1973 and it has resulted in more than eighty thousand interviews for my candidates. It works better than anything you can imagine. So please use it if you want to start getting results, or interviews, as fast you can. It works—don't try to fix it!

So, there you have it. Prepare a statement with features, advantages, and benefits followed by an alternative choice question that will get you the results that you need. Now all you need to do is to practice! You have nothing to lose but your anonymity.

Keeping Track of the Process

This may not come as a surprise, but you absolutely must keep good records of all these calls. Your job search, whether you like it or not, may take six, eight, or nine months. I hope, for your sake, that it doesn't, but you need to be prepared for that possibility. If you follow my advice properly, you're going to talk to numerous people whom you have called many times. Just because a company, or an individual within the company, says there is not an employment opportunity today, it does not mean that there will not be an opportunity in the future.

When you initially cold call like this, your probability of discovering a job vacancy is about one in seventy. You will almost double those odds by calling back a second, third, or fourth time. So, it is important to recognize that cold calling the individual or organization is not simply going to be a one-time thing. Your odds of getting a face-to-face interview at the second or third call are much greater than they were on the first call simply because the person that you're calling is more aware of who you are and what you're doing. Even if it was slight, you made somewhat of an impression on the person the first time you called. By the second, third, or fourth time you call, the person has become more aware of possible employment opportunities that might be available in the organization. If you are going to make the investment of the cold call to begin with, you will reap greater rewards by following it up with subsequent calls.

Simple manila folders can be used to keep records of each organization that you approach or interview with. A daily planner can be used to make notes in every day or into the future. Microsoft Outlook is a great way to keep track of these kinds of records. The alarms keep you from forgetting and if your job search is prolonged, the software is more efficient than paper records.

When people first start out looking to either find or change jobs, they usually have no idea how long it is going to take to be successful. There is a tendency to have a lot of activity in the beginning of the process: However, the process may carry on for a lot longer than a person would imagine. Good record keeping helps the momentum in the beginning to be sustained over however long it takes.

Should You Leave a Voice Mail Message?

Somewhere along the line you're going to be faced with leaving a voice mail message. Unfortunately, more and more business people never answer their phone. Some managers in sales are rarely in their offices and some managers in accounting and engineering departments aren't "people people" anyhow so they let everything go straight to voice mail.

You diligently practice a cold-call presentation and then you get voice mail! So, you ask, "Should I leave a voice mail, or not?" It may be the only way you're going to communicate with many prospective employers.

First off, you should call the same hiring manager at least two or three times, trying to make a presentation to him or her before you leave a message on voice mail. If you conclude, after even the second time, that you're not likely to catch this hiring authority answering the phone, leave a voice mail message.

The phrase you use for the voice mail message isn't much different from the phrase used when a live person answers the phone. The ending, however, is slightly different. It goes like this:

Mr./Ms._____. My name is _____. I am a_____. I have (features) _____ *that are* (advantages) _____, *which would be* (bene-fits) _____ *to you and your firm.*

I would like a chance to meet with you. My phone number is _____. Again, this is _____ (your name), *and my phone number is _____.*

Be sure to repeat your telephone number at the end of the message twice, say it once, and repeat it very s-l-o-w-l-y so the person can write it down as you record it the second time. It might even be advisable to mention your phone number after you state your name in the very first part of your message, so you are offering your phone number three times.

When people have a ton of voice mail messages on their system, they find it tedious to go back and listen to your whole voice mail message a second time. By putting your phone number right after your name in the beginning of your voice mail, you give them a chance to go back to the very beginning of your voice mail, get your phone number, and not have to listen through your whole voice mail just to get your telephone number. If you say it slowly in the beginning of the voice mail and repeat even more slowly at the end of the message, people are more likely to write down the number and return your call.

If you don't get a response the first time you leave a message on voice mail, don't hesitate to record a similar message seven or eight times for the same person. This sounds a bit excessive, but my experience has been that if there is even the slightest pain of needing someone now or in the near future, this kind of message will get the attention of a hiring authority.

You may ask, "Why would I leave that many voice mails for the same thing? If they have a need for what I do, they are going to call me back after the first one, right?" Wrong! The answer is, "No, they aren't!" Well, they might, but it isn't very likely. Here's why: Looking for a job is your highest priority, but the hiring authority has many priorities. Hiring someone may be a top priority one day, but it may drop to priority number twenty-two the next day. If, at the moment the hiring authority gets your voice mail, filling that position is the number one priority, you'll get a callback. If it isn't, you won't.

What's going through the hiring authority's mind? It likely is, "Damn, I really need to fill the job . . . I need to fire Leroy and hire someone else . . . get ready for this surge of business were going to have . . . replace Rhonda because she's going on maternity leave . . . get rid of Ralph because he's late all the time . . . replace Susan because she is transferring to another department. But, I'm late for that meeting. I'll give that guy or gal a call later." And later never comes. The third time you leave a message for the hiring authority, you make it really easy for him or her to pick up the phone and call you back.

There is a tendency for job seekers to think that when a company needs to hire someone, they do it in a thirty-day period or so. People think, "Well, they had an opening a few weeks ago . . . they must've filled it." Based on what I've learned since 1973, I guarantee you it takes more like 120 to 180 days to fill those positions even when the hiring authority says it's high priority. Candidates can be offered jobs, say they'll take them, and then the day before they're supposed to show up, they decline. Or, candidates accept the job, show up, and a week later another opportunity they were considering comes along and is better, so they leave the first job. Maybe the company never finds anybody that they like when they start interviewing, and other things become a higher priority.

Companies begin interviewing candidates, and after a while they decide they want to change their criteria or they don't see anyone that they like and then decide to start all over. The hiring process always takes longer than anyone thinks. Remember, you have everything to win and nothing to lose by leaving a voice mail.

After leaving eight to ten messages similar to this and not getting a response, you should stop calling, at least for now. If your experience has been with a similar kind of organization where your value might be greater than the average candidate looking for a job, you should certainly call back a number of times down the road. But, for now, you should stop calling after eight or ten messages.

If you don't get the courtesy of a callback from a hiring authority, don't take it personally. But you will be surprised at the number of people that call you back simply because they admire your persistence. They'll tell you they don't have an opening, but they appreciate your calling. This is a great opportunity for you to ask for a referral of someone they may know. And again, ask their permission to call back in a month or two.

The In-Person Cold-Call Visit

One great way, and one of the most effective ways, of getting an interview and the attention of a hiring authority (the person with pain) is to simply show up at his or her office and ask the administrative person if you can have a few moments of the hiring authority's time. Then you just wait in the office until he or she sees you.

Once you are meeting the person face-to-face, even if it is a brief moment in the lobby, use this phrase as you hand the person your résumé:

> Mr. or Mrs. _____ (employer), *I understand that you are looking for a candidate to fill your position of* _____. *I am an excellent candidate for that*

job opening and would like to discuss my qualifications with you. Do you have a few moments?

Do not expect that you are going to get an interview right then. That will happen only occasionally. If the hiring authority says that he or she does not have time right then, ask when there will be a better time: Be persistent about setting a specific time. When you have the boldness to do this kind of thing, you have everything to win and nothing to lose.

2

Powerful Phrases for Increasing the Chances Your Résumé Will Get Read

In today's job market, 90 percent of the time you're going to deliver your résumé to an employer by e-mail. Therefore, it is important to know how to craft an e-mail message with powerful words and phrases that will get your résumé read. Once again, the point of delivering a résumé to prospective employers is to obtain an interview. That's true whether you use e-mail or snail mail.

You want to send your résumé to a hiring authority. If you send your résumé to a company's general Web address in response to a job posting, it isn't likely to get into the right hands—that is, the hiring authority feeling the pain, or the person who truly needs to hire someone.

It is best to make your résumé an attachment, rather than a part of the e-mail itself. That way, it's easier for the reader to open, read, and print it.

Unfortunately, if your résumé is sent via an e-mail message, there's a good possibility it may never get read. The time of day that the e-mail arrives in the recipient's inbox, the number of other e-mails the person receives, the person's concerns of the moment, and his or her mood at the time will determine if your e-mail is opened and actually read. If there is urgency in hiring someone, all the e-mails with résumés might be opened. But if the hiring need is low, or if a higher priority has arisen, your e-mail might be ignored or even get deleted. The hiring urgency can ebb and flow, big time. Therefore, your e-mail communication must be short and personal. You need to send an e-mail that addresses the needs of the prospective employer in a concise manner.

The following sections contain some tips for sending an attention-getting e-mail message.

GRAB ATTENTION WITH THE SUBJECT LINE

There is no better place for powerful phrases than in the subject line of an e-mail containing your résumé. Remember that you are communicating directly with the hiring authority—that is, the person with the "pain"—so write subject lines like the following:

Outstanding candidate
150 percent performer
Personally referred by [the person you know]
Proven track record [in the business they are in]
A stable, solid, consistent performer . . .

Or, you can use a phrase or expression that will catch the reader's eye. For example, use a Latin phrase that might be recognized or pique curiosity, such as:

Non illegitimus carborundum.
["Don't let the bastards grind you down."]
Carpe diem.
["Seize the day."]

Omnia mutantur, nos et mutamur in illis.
["All things are changing and we are changing with them."]

If you use this kind of device, though, be sure to briefly explain it in the body of the e-mail, showing how it applies to the position being sought. Similarly, you can use a short quote from a famous person, followed in the body of the e-mail with an analogy to your experience.

The subject line of an e-mail is a chance for you to be creative. Treat it like a newspaper headline or an advertisement. The subject line should grab the reader's attention enough to get him or her to open the e-mail and read it. Be careful, though, that the subject line message isn't so "out there" that the message gets deleted as annoying. For example, "You have just won the lottery," or "News about your distant uncle who left you a fortune," won't get your e-mail message read.

Try different approaches, too. Different personalities respond to different kinds of messages. For instance, a comptroller or a vice president of finance may not be teased into reading an e-mail with a subject line of "Hire a 150 percent performer," but a vice president of sales would. Use your good judgment, but be mindful always of your objective: to get your e-mail résumé opened.

BE AGGRESSIVE, NOT TIMID

Remember, and this is important, that you are trying to motivate the recipient of the e-mail message. It's possible that, within reason, what you might be personally uncomfortable doing may be just the thing that can get you an interview. Over the years, I have recommended that candidates do some fairly aggressive things, either to get an interview or to be remembered after an interview. Some candidates say things like, "Tony, it's 'just not me' to be that aggressive. I'm uncomfortable doing that."

The obvious question is, "Are you more uncomfortable with being *out of work* and not being able to feed your family, or with doing something aggressive that's necessary to find a new job?" If what you're doing isn't getting you the interviews, then you may have to do things that are uncomfortable. You are not being asked to betray your basic beliefs; you are simply trying to get an interview.

I have personally placed almost 10,000 people in new jobs, sometimes by recommending that they do things they feel are either inappropriate or too aggressive. Obviously, this suggestion often works. The point is that you need to look beyond your own needs and consider the recipient's needs, his "pain." Writing a subject line like, "An exceptional candidate needs a job" does not communicate empathy or interest in what the employer wants. Hiring authorities don't care what *you* need. They only care about what *they* need. Now, if you can get what you want by helping them get what they want, everyone is happy.

MAKE THE E-MAIL MESSAGE A QUICK READ

The body of your e-mail message should have the same qualities as a good cover letter: short, personal, and to the point. Consider the recipient and the number of e-mails he or she receives. I personally get between 100 and 150 e-mails a day. If the subject line grabs me, I quickly scan the body of the e-mail. But if the message is more than two or three sentences, I may not read it. The biggest mistake candidates make when e-mailing their résumés is to write long introductions about themselves in an e-mail message.

Instead of going on for paragraphs about your qualifications, tie the body of your e-mail to the subject line in a way that's short, personal, and to the point. Here are a few suggestions:

Subject: "I have lost almost 300 games."
—Michael Jordan

Michael Jordan stated, "I have missed more than 9,000 shots in my career. I have lost almost 300 games. On 26 occasions I have been entrusted to take the game-winning shot and missed. I have failed over and over and over again in my life. And that is why I succeed."

Like Michael Jordan, I know how to succeed. My résumé is attached.

I would like to meet with you and explain my personal "Michael Jordan experiences" and how they would be of value to you and your firm. I will call you tomorrow at 3:00 PM to see when we might get together. Or feel free to reply back and tell me when your schedule might allow us to meet.

Sincerely,

(Your signature and phone number)

• • •

Subject: "Never, never, never quit" —Winston Churchill

Churchill was right. I don't quit.

I understand you and your firm are seeking a quality (accountant, salesperson, engineer, office manager, or other title). I would like to share with you the success I've had and how it will be of value to you and your company.

My résumé is attached. I will call you tomorrow at 10:00 AM to see when it would be convenient for us to get together. Feel free to reply back with a time when your schedule might allow us to meet.

Sincerely,

(Your signature and phone number)

• • •

Subject: Winners do the things losers fail to do

All good companies and leaders are looking for winners. You and your company were referred to me by _____. He said you were an expert in _____ (profession) and would be a great teacher and mentor.

I do the things losers fail to do. At this point in my career, I need a great teacher and mentor.

My résumé is attached. I will call you tomorrow at 1:00 PM to see when we might meet. Or, feel free to reply back with a time when your schedule might allow us to meet.

Sincerely,

(Your signature and phone number)

• • •

Subject: The 200 percent return

The story of how my employer got a 200 percent return on his investment in me is a great one. I can do the same thing for you.

My résumé is attached. When might we be able to meet? I will share with you my story and show how it can apply to you and your firm.

I will call you tomorrow at 10:00 am to arrange a time we might meet. Or, feel free to reply back with a time that it is good for you.

Sincerely,

(Your signature and phone number)

• • •

Subject: *non illigitimus carborundum*

Don't let your board or investors grind you down! You need a hard-working, determined, proven (production engineer, book-keeper, financial analyst, or salesperson) who can withstand the daily grind and the pressure you are under.

My résumé is attached. I will call you tomorrow at 3:00 PM to see when we might be able to meet. Or, feel free to respond to this e-mail with a time that would be convenient for you.

Sincerely,

(Your signature and phone number)

CITE RELEVANT RECENT EVENTS

Another approach along the same lines is to cite information you might have seen about the individual or the company you have researched or discovered, thereby implying that you would be a unique candidate for the company. A recent expansion, or the need for a turnaround, a promotion, or even bankruptcy might make you stand out from the crowd. What follows are some examples.

Subject: Your new plant in Scranton

Congratulations on your company's recent expansion and your being named head of the new plant. I've been closely involved at two companies with getting new facilities successfully up and running.

There is a lot to be done when a company opens a new plant. You and your company may need my hands-on experience in this area. My résumé is attached. I will call you tomorrow morning to see when we might meet.

Sincerely,

(Your signature and phone number)

• • •

Subject: Congratulations on your promotion

I read the announcement of your promotion. From my research, I understand it is well deserved.

Often, when there are changes within a company, new blood may be needed. I have been hired in similar situations three times in my career and have helped leaders, like you, to be tremendously successful.

I will call you tomorrow to see if there's a time we might meet, so I can share with you how I might help you and your organization reach new heights.

Sincerely,

(Your signature and phone number)

• • •

Subject: Your company's reorganization under Chapter 11

Reorganization and Chapter 11 are difficult things to deal with. As a financial specialist, I've helped three companies successfully reorganize.

Your company may need my extensive experience. My résumé is attached along with press releases of the successful Chapter 11 reorganizations that I have led.

I will call you tomorrow morning to see when we might meet.

Sincerely,

(Your signature and phone number)

COVER LETTERS, IF YOU MUST

In a recent survey we conducted with hiring authorities, we found that most cover letters are read only when the hiring authority has already read your résumé and wants to know more about you.

Remember, since your résumé is going to get read in ten to thirty seconds, you can assume that your cover letter isn't going to get much more attention and probably will get less. You are trying to sell the potential employer on the idea of granting you a face-to-face interview, not on hiring you. Even if your cover letter gives all the reasons you ought to be hired, you're going to have to get interviewed anyway. So, it is important to sell yourself only one step at a time—in this case, your cover letter and your résumé are written to secure the interview.

Remember the principles for Web communication as stated by Facebook's founder, Mark Zuckerberg: seamless, informal, immediate, personal, simple, minimal, and short. A cover letter, therefore, should have the following characteristics:

→ Be short and to the point (especially if you send it electronically).

→ Encourage the hiring authority to interview you.

→ List your accomplishments that apply to the specific job opening.

→ Use bullet points to attract attention.

➜ Sign personally (with an electronic signature, if necessary).

➜ Always have a postscript that is an "action item" (it will get read before the body of the letter does).

I can't tell you the number of résumés I receive with a full-page cover letter that will rarely, if ever, get read. Remember, the screening or interviewing authority has, on average, sixty of these résumés and cover letters to review (even after sorting through 100 or more). You have to make an impact quickly, with specifics that say: "You need to interview me."

Here are two sample cover letters with appropriate powerful words and phrases.

Cover Letter #1

If possible, have a personal phone conversation with the hiring authority and then send your résumé with a brief cover letter to act as a reminder. In this case, you've established rapport and your letter and résumé will be more likely to get read. A typical cover letter of this type should look something like this:

Dear John,

Thank you for the time we spent on the phone. Based on what we discussed, I would be an excellent candidate for the position of accounting manager.

Attached is my résumé. You stated you were looking for someone who:

- Was a CPA with ten years of experience in the insurance industry
- Has managed a staff of a least five accountants

- Has experience with properties and casualties, as well as life, accident, and health
- Has a clear track record of making difficult decisions

As you can see from my résumé:

- I've been a CPA and have twelve years of experience in the insurance industry.
- I have managed as many as five degreed accountants; overall, there was a staff of ten people.
- I've had three years of properties and casualties, as well as eight years of life, accident, and health.
- I have a clear track record of making difficult decisions, especially in the firm I worked for last; we had to close five offices and lay off thirty-five people in order to be profitable.

Sincerely,
(Your signature and phone number)

P.S.: I will call you tomorrow at 1:30 PM about meeting with you this week.

It's that simple. Don't make your cover letter any more complicated or longer than this sample. Use three or four short bullet points with as many quantifiable statements as possible. Then ask for an appointment.

Cover Letter #2

If you don't have the luxury of a phone conversation beforehand, you might use the information you gathered from a job posting or just plain old common sense. Your letter might look something like this:

Dear Mr. Smith,

I understand you are searching for a general manager for your building products distributorship. Attached is my résumé. As you can see:

- I've grown a building-products distributorship from $10 million in sales with a 2 percent pretax profit to $100 million in sales with a 5 percent pretax profit.
- I started out on the ground floor in sales, then moved to sales management, then to general management over a period of fifteen years.
- I offer stability; I've had only two employers in those fifteen years.
- The owners of my previous firm will testify that they were able to successfully sell the organization because of my leadership.

Sincerely,
(Your signature and phone number)

P.S.: I will call you tomorrow at 1:30. We can make an appointment to meet.

P.S.S.: Enclosed (or attached) are the results of a psychological profile our company did on all of its managers. You can see that I scored in the upper 2 percent of all managers the consulting firm surveyed on a worldwide basis.

PERSONAL AND SPECIFIC = POWERFUL

Words and phrases that communicate personal connection are very powerful. So begin a cover letter or e-mail with statements like:

> *We both graduated from Stanford . . .*
> *We were both members of Sigma Chi . . .*
> *We both worked at XYZ Corp a few years ago . . .*
> *We both know . . .*

These will encourage the recipient to read a little further.

Remember. Powerful words and phrases should be specific and as quantifiable as possible. Numbers are great because they are definite. Writing "I'm a great performer" is fine, but writing "I performed at 150 percent of quota," or "I have received the highest marks . . . 100 out of 100 . . . in performance reviews," really makes a big difference. Remember the adage: "Stories sell . . . numbers tell." Only use numbers when they are high. Writing something like "performed at 50 percent of quota" is not powerful.

OTHER ATTACHMENTS TO YOUR RÉSUMÉ

Some job candidates send other attachments with their résumés that further substantiate their success. As with the résumé and cover letter, these should be relatively short and obvious. At a glance they should communicate, "My résumé and cover letter state that I am a very successful business person—here is proof of that."

What kind of information might you attach? You might include:

→ A positive performance or salary review

→ Previously published documents of former employers ranking your performance as high

→ Personal psychological evaluations that show high rankings in leadership

→ Personality surveys that indicate you are a strong salesperson or analytical thinker

→ News releases of recognition and honors

→ Thirty-, sixty-, or ninety-day plans you have developed in the past or would implement if you got hired

Any objective document that substantiates your success—as long as it is concise and clear when viewed—will work. Often these attachments get viewed before the résumé is read.

A few of our candidates, not having this kind of objective proof of their skills, have gone online and taken self-administered psychological, intelligence, and aptitude tests. They pay for these tests and get formal results. If they perform well, they attach the results to their résumés.

I had one candidate who took two intelligence tests showing he was in the upper 2 percent of the surveyed population regarding intelligence. He also took three sales aptitude tests that proved he was in the upper 5 percent of sales performers, and a leadership survey that proved he was a strong leader. He got tons of interviews because of these attachments.

Anything that separates you from the average candidate can be attached. One of our candidates attached a link to the Amazon.com page of her published book of poetry.

Be sure to conclude each communication with the prospective employer, either an e-mail or a cover letter, with the powerful phrase:

When can we get together?

3

Powerful Phrases for Opening and Closing the Initial Interview

The job interview is a staged, contrived event. It does not have anything to do with your ability to do a job. Although the job interview is supposedly a mutual evaluation of your past record and talents and a prediction of how you're going to perform in the future, as well as your personal evaluation of the hiring organization, it is rarely any of these things.

Each party in this process is putting his or her best foot forward, and rightfully so. Candidates are responsible for selling themselves to the employer, trying to convince the employer that they are the best person for the job. The company (or the individuals representing it) is trying to find the best person to do the job while both selling the merits of the company and screening out the candidates it does not think will be capable of doing the job or fitting in.

As a job candidate, your job is to communicate the following: that you can do the job; that you are likable; that you offset any risks that you pose to the company; and that you are reasonable about the compensation. That's it! For you as a candidate, it is no more complicated than answering those questions. That is the essence of the interviewing process. It is very simple—just not very easy.

All of your experience, achievements, and knowledge won't matter unless you can sell yourself in the interviewing process. What this means is that, in spite of the fact that interviewing is a staged, contrived event, it is absolutely necessary that it be done, and done well. The better your ability to interview is, the better your opportunity to get a good job.

And it all starts with the first interview! Having the right words and phrases at your command during the initial interview will give you the confidence and clarity to set yourself apart from the other candidates.

SUCCESSFUL INITIAL INTERVIEW TECHNIQUE #1

You walk into the interviewer's office or interviewing environment. You are rested, refreshed, and prepared. You sit down and lean forward a bit. After you share a few icebreakers, you pull out a legal pad and pen to take notes, you hand the hiring or interviewing authority your résumé (even if he or she already has it), and state:

> *Mr. or Ms. _____, I'm here to share with you why you should hire me. First of all, I am _____*
>
> _____
>
> (choose ten to twelve descriptive adjectives to explain your work ethic).

You've introduced yourself by providing a quick overview of your credentials (features). Now you transition into specifics:

Now here in my background is where these features have been benefits to the people whom I have worked for:

_____

_____

_____

_____.

Give a thorough description of exactly what you did, how you did it, whom you did it for, and how successful you were—in terms a high-school senior could understand.

I am presently (or most recently have been) *at* _____ (company). *I have functioned for them in the capacity of*

_____.

You then emphasize how much you love the job and the company, and explain the reason you have to leave or why you left in very positive terms.

I like the company very much. I enjoy the work I do and the people I work with, but I feel that my chances for advancement have been greatly reduced by the number of new managers who have recently been brought into the company.

Continue on through your work history, again giving a thorough description of exactly what you did, how you did it, whom you did it for, and how successful you were—in terms a high-school senior could understand.

And before that, I was at _____ (company). *There, I functioned in the capacity of* _____

_____.

Here, too, emphasize how much you loved that job and why you had to leave it in very positive terms.

> *I loved working there. The job was very interesting, and I was surrounded by bright, capable people. Unfortunately, my boss left the company and his replacement brought in several of his own people. As a result, I felt it was time to move on.*

Continue in this manner for at least three jobs, if you have that many. If you've had a series of short stints at jobs, like one year or less, you may want to go back further than three jobs.

Ask Questions and Gather Information

Now you want to start discussing the specific job at hand and how good a fit it is for you:

> *Tell me Mr. or Ms. _____, how does what I have to offer stack up with what you are looking for?*

With the legal pad in front of you, start taking notes on how the interviewer answers this question and begin to ask other questions of the interviewer. If you do this correctly, one question will lead to another question, which will lead to another question, which will lead to a conversation, which is exactly what you want.

During this conversation, the hiring or interviewing authority is going to tell you more about what the company is looking for in an individual. When the interviewer does this, you can weave into the conversation any important information on yourself that pertains to the company and the job.

You say communication skills are important in doing this job. At ABC Company, I had to keep channels open with my peers and with management. I was praised for my ability to communicate with both groups.

Also expand upon the information you've provided about where you have been, what you have done, and how you did it.

It's interesting that you mention the need to coordinate the work of the tech people with that of the creative team. When I was with XYZ Company, I served as a conduit between IT and Creative to make sure the work was compatible.

As the conversation/interview winds down, when you feel the time is appropriate, it's time to use these powerful phrases (as mentioned in the Introduction):

Based on what we have discussed here, Mr. or Ms. _____, my (background, experience, or potential) *_____ makes this a good fit for both of us.*

   How do I stack up with the other candidates you have interviewed?

   What do I need to do to get the job?

Then be quiet and don't say a word.

Now, the conversation may go off in a number of different directions. If you have to repeat your enthusiasm and interest in the position, you may need to push harder and repeat the fact that you are an ideal candidate for the job and you want to know what you have to do to get it.

Analysis of Interview Technique #1

Let's analyze this technique, and then I'll tell you why it works so well. (It's based on a powerful persuasion method used by salespeople and speakers alike to get their point across and make sure they are remembered. That method is: "Tell 'em what you're gonna tell 'em . . . tell 'em . . . then, tell 'em what you told 'em.")

What you say up front is really simple. You state ten to twelve basic intangible traits of a hard-working, successful, committed worker that you possess. In the final analysis, all hiring or interviewing authorities want to see is somebody who is going to possess the traits of a committed, hard-working employee.

Mr. or Ms., I'm here to share with you why you should hire me. First of all, I am: _____
(choose ten to twelve descriptive adjectives to explain your work ethic).

What you're doing in this phase is simply communicating that you understand what hard work is. You would be shocked and amazed at the number of people who go into an interviewing situation and just assume that the interviewing or hiring authority already knows that they are a committed worker. Remember that your hiring or interviewing authority is scared of making a mistake. This person is afraid of risk.

When you communicate the ten to twelve intangible traits of a hard worker that you possess, it provides assurance in the interviewer's cautious state that you not only know what the traits of a hard worker are, but also that you possess them. What I recommend here is stressing traits such as:

hard worker
determined to go the extra mile

accomplished

intelligent

passionate about my work

committed to the customer

love what I do

get in early, stay late

great work ethic

I cannot emphasize enough that prospective employers hardly ever hear these words from the typical candidate. You are simply communicating basic attributes that every employer wishes he or she saw in every employee.

The transition phrase leading to the next part of your presentation is:

Now, here in my background is where these features have been benefits to the people I have worked for.

You are using the terms *features* and *benefits*. It is implied that these features will be benefits to the hiring authority and his or her company. This transition phrase allows you to lead into an explanation of every job you have had, what you've done, how you've done it, and how successful you were.

You are doing their thinking for them! They don't need to ask that stupid question, "Well, tell me about yourself." (The worst question you can get asked.)

At this point, you are going to work backwards and give a short, but very thorough, description about exactly what job function you had, how you did it, who you did it for, and how successful you were, as well as—and this is very important—that you loved the job and why, in very positive terms, you're looking to leave or why you left. The execution of this phase of your presentation is very important. There are clear key parts to this phase: explaining your job function, explaining why you want to leave the job, and telling stories about what you have done.

Explain your job function. First of all, you need to explain *exactly* what your job function is now or was in the past so that the hiring or interviewing authority understands *exactly* what you have done before. I can't tell you the number of times over the years that candidates have walked away from interviews thinking that they had done a really good job on the interview—only to have the hiring authority, in giving us feedback, explain that he or she really didn't understand what the candidate did (either in his present job or the jobs he had before).

Give a thorough description of exactly what you did, how you did it, whom you did it for, and how successful you were—in terms a high-school senior could understand:

> At _____ (company), *I was in charge of inventory control. As soon as the in-house supply of an item reached a predetermined level, I made sure a new supply was ordered immediately. I reported to the store manager. In my three years at that position, we never ran out of an item.*

Hiring authorities are just as nervous as you are in the interviewing process. They feel like they have to get a deeper understanding about you and your background in order to evaluate you. They usually have to do this with a large number of people. Most of the time in the interviewing process, when a hiring or interviewing authority asks a question, partway through your answer they are thinking about the next question, and then partway through that answer, they're thinking about the next question, and so forth.

On top of that, most hiring or interviewing authorities don't want to look stupid or ignorant. Like most people, they are uncomfortable saying, "I don't understand, could you explain it to me in layman's terms so that I really get it?" After all, they are the hiring authority. They are supposed to know and understand everything as the so-called authority. So, they will act like they know exactly what the candidate is talking about, and nod their head in complete agreement and understanding as the candidate speaks in terms foreign to everyone but himself.

Then, after the candidate leaves, rather than admitting they had no idea what the hell the candidate was talking about, they will claim that the candidate's skills, experience, background, or personality aren't what they were looking for.

Explain why you want to leave your job. Next, you need to explain, in very positive ways, why you are seeking to leave the company you're with now and why you left other jobs. I cannot overemphasize this point. You are going to weave into your explanation, along with what you've done and how you have done it, all of the positive reasons that you left the companies and the jobs that you had or the one that you are leaving now.

> *I have learned a tremendous amount at this job. However, I feel that it's time to take my talents and new skills to another level. It doesn't seem like I have much room for advancement where I am.*

If you bring up why you left in positive terms—even if it wasn't under the most positive circumstances (for example, you were fired)—the whole scenario has a tendency to be more palatable to a hiring authority.

Although I was quite successful at _____ *(com-pany), they hit some hard times and had to let people go. I was the most recent hire in my department, so I was laid off. The manager said I would be brought back if a job opened up.*

This is going to take much thought and practice on your part. You always want to tell the truth; but you might have to put a spin on it, that, if nothing else, neutralizes any negative connotations. Do not think that an interviewing or hiring authority is going to see things from your personal point of view. Trying to justify your getting fired, or quitting on a whim, the awful environment you were in, the lousy boss, the lousy pay, the lousy CEO, your stupid peers, the "going nowhere" job, and so on, will do nothing but hurt you. Communicate your positive feelings about previous employers . . . and if you can't immediately think of any . . . think harder!

You are also going to communicate in the second phase that you absolutely loved every job you ever had. You don't have to use the word *love* in every instance. But you need to communicate that you had a very positive experience with every job that you have ever had; that you learned a lot from each one; and that you really appreciated the people you worked for. You can communicate this by saying things like:

You know I really love the organization that I work for now but unfortunately . . .

In this phase of your presentation, you only need to go back maybe three or, at the most, four jobs and describe what I have suggested here. If you had jobs before that, unless they are germane to the position that you are presently applying for, you can lump them together by just saying something like:

Before that (meaning the third or fourth position back), *I was in sales or accounting or engineering* (insert your job area) *for a number of different firms.*

You want to make sure that you don't ramble for so long that the interviewing or hiring authority gets bored. Stick to the high points in your background that are applicable to the job for which you are interviewing. It should not take more than five to seven minutes.

Tell stories. It's very important to weave many stories about what you have done as examples of your successes. People love stories. People remember stories. People remember you when you tell them stories about your past. Stories bypass conscious resistance and preconceived notions. Stories, analogies, and metaphors about you that pertain to the hiring authority's need are absolutely the best way to be remembered. Of course, they need to be short, to the point, and above all pertinent to the opportunity for which you were interviewing.

When leading into a story that appropriately fits the discussion, say to the interviewer something like:

That reminds me of the time I had to fill in for the floor supervisor when he was out sick for several weeks.

We once had a strike at the plant that supplied the rubber wheels for our carts.

I worked with a person who absolutely refused to do anything that fell outside the strict parameters of her job.

Once you've set the stage this way, you can transition smoothly into the story demonstrating how you successfully handled a specific situation:

A number of years ago, we had a candidate who held an engineering degree from Texas A&M. He was born and raised on a chicken farm, which he noted on his résumé. Subsequently, in interviews, he told stories about his childhood on the chicken farm—how hard the work was, what he learned, and so on. The company that hired him admitted that what made him stand out from the other candidates was that his stories gave them confidence that he would be a hard worker.

The transition phrase leading to the next part of your presentation is:

Tell me, Mr. or Ms. _____, how does what I have to offer stack up with what you are looking for?

This is a powerful phrase that leads to the next stage of your initial interview technique: asking questions and gathering information. This is one the most important power phrases you will use in the initial interview. It is designed to get interviewers or hiring authorities to tell you exactly what they are looking for and, more importantly, how your skills and experience stack up with your competition.

I can't emphasize the importance of this question enough. Candidates are always impressed with the reaction that they get from most interviewing and hiring authorities. It is a courageous question and gives you exactly what you need to know.

Asking Questions and Gathering Information

This is a crucial phase of the initial interview, where you begin to dig deeper into the details of what the company is looking for, how well you fit, and who your competition is. When the interviewing or hiring authority starts answering your question of how you stack up with what he or she is looking for, take notes. When the interviewer stops answering that question, you want to have a prepared set of questions ready.

Some questions that you may ask are:

What are the most important qualities that a successful person in this position should possess?

How would you measure the success of the last person that was in this job?

Why was he or she successful? or *Why was he or she not successful?*

In your opinion, what is the most difficult part of the job?

Mr. or Ms._____, how long have you been with the company?

Why do you like working here?

What is the most difficult part of your job?

I could go on and on, but you get the idea. Ask enough questions to engage the employer or hiring authority in the conversation. You want this person to open up to you as much as he or she possibly can about what they want in the person they are going to hire. You then have a better idea of how to sell yourself into the job.

The following is very important. As the conversation progresses and you write down some of the highlights of what the employer is looking for, you will reinforce the fact that you are a qualified, excellent candidate by going back to some of the jobs that you had, or the job you presently have, and talk in even more specific terms than before. As the interviewing or hiring authority is sharing with you his or her exact needs, you need to be able to relate exact experience, responsibilities, duties, and successes that you have had that *specifically* address the particular issues being discussed:

> *I agree with you that quality is the number-one priority. When I worked at _____, I always made sure to check my figures twice. To me, there's nothing worse than making a mistake that could have been avoided with a little extra effort.*

In the presentation you made, you talked about each job that you either currently have or have had, your duties and responsibilities, and your successes. But you did it in a very broad, descriptive way. Now you are going to use the information that the interviewing or hiring authority is giving you and bring up examples in your current job or your previous jobs that specifically demonstrate your ability to do the job under consideration. Whereas your initial presentation about your experience and background was detailed enough for the interviewing or hiring authority to understand what you have done, you now get specific about particular things that would be of value to the interviewing or hiring authority based on the conversation that results from the questions you ask:

> *You say there's a need to take action when a project is running late. I never feel right when things fall behind schedule. I do all I can—come in early, stay late, work weekends—to get the job back on track.*

After the conversation has begun to wind down and you can see that the interview is nearly over, you close by stating that your background and experience fit what the employer is looking for, and then you need to ask:

What do I need to do to get the job?

This is the hardball part of the interview. You are either a candidate or you're not, and you need to know right now!

This is one of the hardest phrases to get candidates to use. I hear it from candidates, from radio callers, and from my own candidates: After I have instructed them to ask this question, even after they have agreed to ask it, they don't. They will even admit, "I know I should have asked, but it didn't seem appropriate . . ."; that is, "I was just too darn scared to ask . . . afraid they'd simply tell me I wasn't going to be considered." Listen to me: "No" is the second-best answer you can get. More often than not at this point in the interview, most candidates are going to fear "no" so much, they avoid the rejection.

Interviewing and hiring authorities want to hire an individual who wants the job. I cannot tell you the number of candidates over the years that failed to ask this essential question in the interview and ended up being dismissed by the interviewing or hiring authority. I know that this is terribly unfair. But life is unfair. This is a part of the interview that truly is a contrived event. The truth is, there is no real way of knowing whether or not you really want this job right now. But, unless you ask for the job, you're never going to get beyond first base.

Whatever you do, don't fall into the trap of thinking, "Well, I'm not really sure that I want the job so, before I commit, I better think about it." Remember, while you are thinking about it, somebody else is getting an offer. You don't have anything to decide about until you have an offer.

Asking "what do I need to do to get the job?" takes courage. That's okay. But if you're serious about finding a job, you will use this question at the end of every interview, especially the initial one.

SUCCESSFUL INITIAL INTERVIEW TECHNIQUE #2

This technique is for those people who feel more comfortable with trying to find out what an interviewing or hiring authority might be interested in *before* they talk about their experience. That way, they have some advance warning and can start formulating their thoughts ahead of time on what they will say as the interview progresses. It seems to work best with analytical types of hiring authorities who are not sales oriented: accountants, finance people, and information technology folks.

It isn't much different than the first technique, except that you ask the question about what they are looking for before you talk about your intangible attributes and other experiences and background. Here's how it works.

You sit down in the interviewing or hiring authority's office, take a deep breath, and after the pleasantries (as you put the legal pad down in front of you), you say:

Tell me, Mr. or Ms. _____, what kind of candidate would you ideally like to find?

As the hiring or interviewing authority speaks, you take notes about what they're looking for in an ideal candidate. You may ask a number of questions, but the idea is to find out—in the employer's words—what they're looking for. Then you can start matching your skills and experience to the job opening:

If you will allow me, Mr. or Ms._____, I would like to explain why I would fit what you are looking for and how I could do the job.

First of all, I am _____

_____ (ten to twelve descriptive adjectives to explain your work ethic).

Now is the time to start selling yourself as a candidate:

Based on what you said you wanted in a candidate, I would like to demonstrate where these features have been beneficial to the people whom I've worked for, in the light of what you need.

I am currently (or most recently have been) at _____ (company). I have functioned for them in the capacity of _____

_____

_____.

Give a thorough description of exactly what you did, how you did it, whom you did it for, and how successful you were—in terms a high-school senior could understand. You then emphasize how much you love the job and the company and the reason you have to leave or why you left in very positive terms. Tell a story or two.

And before that, I was at _____ (company). There, I functioned in the capacity of _____

_____.

Again, give a thorough description of exactly what you did, how you did it, whom you did it for, and how successful you were.

I was the assistant to the top buyer. I accompanied her on all trips to locate new merchandise. We discussed the pros and cons of all new items before making a final purchasing decision. The store enjoyed 10 percent growth in each of my first two years there, and 20 percent growth in my last year.

You then emphasize how much you love the job and the company and the reason you have to leave or why you left in very positive terms. Tell a story, if appropriate.

I loved my work there, and I learned so much working with my boss. I would have stayed, but the company was bought out by a competitor, and they had their own team of buyers.

Continue on with your job history, building the story of your experience:

And before that, I was at _____ (company). There I functioned in the capacity of _____
_____.
That was more an entry-level position, learning the ropes from some of the best people in the field. When a better opportunity with more chance for advancement came along, I felt I had to take a chance and move on. But I'll always fondly remember those early days at _____ (company).

Continue in this manner for at least three jobs, if you have that many. If you've had a series of short stints at jobs—like more than one in the last year or less—you may want to go back further than three jobs.

Note that the only difference between this and the first technique is that you ask up front what the employer is looking for in an ideal candidate. With this approach, you might be able to be more specific about the things that the employer wants in a candidate in the descriptions of the jobs that you had.

The drawback to this technique is that the hiring authority may drive the conversation. You may not get the chance to make your presentation because the hiring authority is directing the interview. Use your own judgment.

CLOSING THE INITIAL INTERVIEW WITH POWERFUL PHRASES

Once you and the hiring or interviewing authority have reached the end of the interview, you're probably going to get some idea of what the next steps might be. Don't be afraid to be assertive about pushing yourself into the next steps of the interviewing process:

> *Based on what you said you wanted, I'm an excellent match.*

Remember, the two most important and powerful questions you can ask are:

> *How do I stack up with the other candidates you have interviewed?*

> *What do I need to do to get the job?*

Most often, even though you have pushed for the next interview, a hiring or interviewing authority is going to say something like, "Well, we have a number of people to interview, we're going to complete that process and then we're going to set up second interviews."

This is a perfect time for you to use the following phrase:

Based on what our conversation has been here, I would think that I would be in that group, would I not? So let's set up that second interview now.

Then you pull out your note pad or calendar and ask:

When would be good for me to come back?

You will probably still get from the interviewing or hiring authority the standard, "We'll get in touch with you." Again, this is an excellent time for you to find out how you really stand, relative to the other candidates with this powerful phrase:

Well, Mr. or Ms._____, you must have some idea how I stack up with your ideal candidate or the others whom you have interviewed. Please tell me what you think.

These kinds of questions (and statements) will usually get you a good idea of how you stand. It is relatively aggressive, and it does not necessarily come naturally or easily. But if you practice asking these kinds of hardball questions, they will wind up becoming very easy for you.

You may use a different phrase to get the same answer:

Based on the candidates that you have interviewed, do you think I'm going to be one of the finalists?

This is a phenomenal question to ask. It takes lots of courage, and most candidates, unfortunately, don't have that kind of courage

Another powerful phrase you can use at this time is:

I consider my strengths concerning this position to be . . .
(my experience . . . my knowledge of your business). *What do you consider my strengths to be?*

AFTER THE INTERVIEW

The first thing you should do after the interview, when you get into your car, is take out the notes you took during the interview and write down a summary of the interview. Write down the high points of the interview and the major issues or topics that you spoke with the interviewer about. Summarize for yourself where you think your strengths are and where you think your weaknesses are—relative to the interview. Write down your interpretation of the things that seemed the most important to the hiring authority and make sure that you understand them clearly.

Often, in the initial interviewing situation, we think we completely understand what a hiring authority is looking for, and we actually do not! The major reason you want to collect your thoughts immediately after the interview is so that you remember the important points; you cannot rely on your memory. It may be a two- to four-week period of time before the second round of interviews. You need to be able to refresh your memory with detailed notes.

The Immediate E-Mail

You have gotten the business card of the interviewing or hiring authority at the time of the interview. Immediately after the interview, or as soon as possible, you want to e-mail the interviewing or hiring authority. You don't just want to thank the person for his or her time. More important, you want to reinforce all the reasons that you should be hired.

Every interviewing book in the world is going to tell you to send a thank-you to the interviewer. You would probably be shocked at the number of candidates who don't do this. One out of every seven or eight, even when they're coached by a professional, either don't do it or do it so long after the interview that it is ineffective. Of course, thanking someone for the interview is obviously important. But what is most important is that you reinforce the high points of what the interviewing or hiring authority said he or she wanted and restate where or how you address those issues better than anyone else.

The phrases you use in this e-mail need to be short and to the point. Do not ramble about how much you appreciated the interview, how much you like the person, or how you appreciate the conversation. This e-mail is going to be read, like the résumé, in ten seconds. So this is what it should look like (remember to make it look like an actual letter):

Dear Mr. or Ms. _____,

Thank you for taking the time to speak with me today, regarding the position with _____. Your needs and my qualifications are compatible. You stated that you wanted someone who has:

- (Experience or attributes that the employer said were wanted.)

- (Another experience or attribute the employer said were wanted.)
- (Another experience or attribute the employer said were wanted.)

I have given a lot of thought to what we spoke about. I would like to reinforce the confidence you can have in me to deliver what you need.

- When I was at _____ (company) last year, I (accomplished the first thing that you wrote about for experience).
- Before that, when I was at _____ (company), I (accomplished or proved the second thing you wrote about).
- And, when I was at _____ (company), I (accomplished or proved the third thing you wrote about).

I'm an excellent fit for you and your company. I would like to go to work for you and your firm. This is a win/win situation for both of us.

Sincerely,

(Your name and phone number)

When you reinforce what the interviewing or hiring authorities say they want, you need to do it in quantifiable terms. State things that can be measured objectively, such as percentages of quota, longevity on the job, grades in school, stability, being promoted consistently—anything that can be measured in a quantitative manner. Make sure that you address specific issues that the interviewing or hiring authority stated were of value to them.

Follow-Up Phone Call

A follow-up phone call the day after your initial interview can be very effective and it is a perfect opportunity to use powerful phrases. If you get the interviewing hiring authority on the phone—and that's only going to happen maybe 10 percent of the time—you want to use a phrase like:

> *Mr. or Ms._____, Thank you for your time yesterday. I really enjoyed the opportunity to interview with you. I want to reinforce my interest in you and your company. I think I would be a great employee for you because* _____ (some really important point that you learned from the interview that would set you apart from the rest of the candidates). *I'd like the opportunity to visit with you again. When might we get together?*

Most people don't think about this kind of phone call, but it is tremendously effective. You probably will not get the hiring or interviewing authority on the phone, so you'll have to leave a voice mail. The phrase to use for the voice mail might be:

> *Mr. or Ms._____, thank you for the interview and the time you gave to me yesterday. I'm very excited about the opportunity to go to work for you and your company. Please remember that I am a very hard worker and my track record in _____ would really help you and your company. I'd like to come back and speak with you again. Please call me at 214-823-9999.*

If you do not hear back from the interviewing or hiring authority, it's a good idea to leave this kind of voice mail at least five or six times, maybe with a bit different message each time, over a period of two or three weeks. But don't hesitate to leave these kinds of messages. The interviewing process never goes as fast as most people think, and you want to keep the attention of the interviewing or hiring authority.

Most hiring authorities don't intentionally think, "I'm not gonna call those suckers back. They're schmucks, and I'm not going to hire them anyhow." The truth is that their intentions to do what they are supposed to do are sincere, but the activity just doesn't get done. The process of hiring often slips further behind in favor of other more pressing, less risky, issues. So, a timely call, and many of them after that—if you have to—may put you on top of the list of potential candidates.

Now, after ten to fifteen days of calling an interviewing or hiring authority, with no response at all, you might wind up with the conclusion that you should pursue other people and other opportunities. Never, never, never take this result personally and do something stupid, like calling the hiring authority and leaving a mean, sarcastic voice mail about what they can do with the job and that you didn't want it anyhow. There is often a tendency to take perceived rejection personally.

The odds are that if you have not heard from a prospective employer in a couple of weeks, you were probably not on the list of candidates to be considered. But you never really know. Always leave the door open, so that if a prospective employer wants to still consider you, even after weeks or months have gone by, you could resurrect the opportunity.

You never know what might happen. I can't tell you the number of people that I've placed over the years that have come in second or third in the hiring process and wound up getting the job. The company hires somebody and after a short period of time it doesn't work out. Then they call the number two candidate.

Some years ago, I had a candidate who came in second place. The company was so impressed with his credentials that they considered him for another opportunity and hired him . . . seven years later. Always be gracious, even if you were told "no." You never know what might happen down the line.

4 Powerful Phrases to Demonstrate Your Ability to Do the Job

One of the biggest concerns in the mind of a hiring authority is the fear of making a mistake. Mistakes cost the company time and money and can affect the credibility of the person doing the hiring.

No matter how sophisticated the interviewing process might be, hiring someone is still something of a crapshoot. You need to realize that since the hiring authority is trying to minimize risk, there are certain basic questions that they will want answered to their satisfaction. Your job in the interviewing process is to assure the hiring authority that he or she is not making a mistake— there will be no risk in hiring you.

There are four basic questions that are the cornerstones of every question you will get in an interview. It could be the first interview with a screener or the ninth interview with the CEO. You will not be asked any of these four questions outright during the interview, but they are there just below the surface. Employers want satisfactory answers to all four of the following questions before they will hire you:

1. Can you do the job?
2. Do we like you?
3. Are you a risk?
4. Can we work the money out?

You need to have powerful phrases that are also short responses for every question the hiring or interviewing authority will ask you. You can elaborate beyond the phrase—especially with stories—but having an initial response with impact sets the stage for a more detailed answer, if necessary.

CAN YOU DO THE JOB?

Of the four basic questions, the one an employer wants answered before anything else is "Can you do the job?" You need to be able to demonstrate your skills, ability, and experience. You might be surprised by this, but I have found that the ability to do the job is only about 20 percent of the hiring decision. However, it is the *first* 20 percent, the threshold that you have to cross before you can even be considered—and that's significant; but it still only accounts for about 20 percent.

Now, having said this, you still have to establish your ability to do the job. And this is the very first group of questions you will get. If you don't answer them well, you may not get to the other questions. These are going to be factual "What did you do?" questions. The interviewing authority is trying to discover your skill level or potential. There are going to be only four or five factual aspects of your work history that will either get you to the second interviewing stage or eliminate you. Remember, just four or five facts will either support or conflict with what you say you can do.

Following are the most frequently asked questions on your ability to do the job and the most effective phrases to use as answers.

QUESTIONS ON YOUR JOB EXPERIENCE

Needless to say, interviewers will be especially interested in your job history, what you've done, what you've learned, where you've succeeded, and where you've fallen short.

Q. Tell me about yourself and your last few jobs.

In all of my recent positions, I've been successful in contributing to my company's profitability.

Q. Describe in detail what you do in your current job (or in your last position).

I really love the job that I'm in now (or the last job I had) *because I really get to contribute by_____* (then explain in fair detail what you do or what you did).

When you are done, ask the interviewer this question:

Did I make it clear what I do (did)*?*

Q. What percentage of your week or month was devoted to the different functions of your job?

Twenty percent administrative, 30 percent management, and 50 percent collaborative effort with my team.

Q. What was the most difficult part of your last two jobs?

Even though _____ was the most difficult part of the job, I met the challenge every time.

Adding a short story as to how you overcame a difficult challenge in each one of your last jobs really works well.

Q. Describe the best job that you've ever had . . . and why it was so much better than others.

There have been some wonderful aspects to just about every job I've had. I have really loved all of them, and they are all best for different reasons.

This is a powerful way to lead into your answer.

Q. What is your greatest accomplishment in your present or last job?

Because I was given a chance to perform 110 percent over what was expected, I grew professionally and personally.

You are going to get asked this question by just about everyone you interview with, so prepare. Hiring authorities love when you can quantify your success.

Q. What specifically have you learned from the jobs that you held most recently?

In my present position, my persistence (determination, earning respect, loyalty, and so on) *was reinforced when the group I led tried five or six approaches to a problem before we solved it. Most people would have stopped at two or three.*

Tell another short, effective story.

Q. In what way has your present job prepared you to take on greater responsibilities? (You'd better have an answer to this question before it ever gets asked.)

I love my job and the people I work with. Unfortunately, I've reached a point now where I can do my boss's job. Even he has said that. But he isn't going anywhere and doesn't plan to retire for another ten years. To move up in the company, I'd have to relocate.

I'm not bored, but I'm not challenged either. That is why I am interviewing with you all. It appears I can really be challenged here.

Q. Describe a difficult business problem that you had to deal with and how you handled it?

In my last (one, two, . . .) *jobs, I had to either fire for cause* (or lay people off). *It was hard. I was successful in doing it gracefully, benefitting my company, and with little rancor on the part of the employees I had to let go.*

Q. Describe the situation in your last one or two jobs where you made a mistake. What was the mistake and how did you rectify it? (Be ready to provide a hindsight type of answer. Give the example, but highlight what you learned from it. Have one or two of these kinds of stories available for this question when you get it.)

In my present position, we lost a very good employee. Look-
ing back on it, she left for reasons I might have been able to
fix if I had realized the situation before it was too late.

If I had to do it again, I would've been more aware of the
situation before she left.

Whatever you do, don't say that you haven't made any mistakes that you can recall. That sounds disingenuous. Talk about
a challenge and what you learned from it.

**Q. Where have you made difficult decisions before and what
were they about?** (In the last economic downturn, there were
probably some difficult financial or personnel decisions you
had to make. Think of one and put it into a one- or two-sentence
phrase.)

I had to cut $152,000 from my budget and lay off two peo-
ple. Everyone on the team had been a good employee. It was
a difficult decision.

**Q. Have you ever had to fire someone? Describe the circum-
stances?**

Firing people is one of the most difficult tasks that a man-
ager has. But I found that if one does it in a very careful,
well-documented, reasonable, businesslike manner, although
uncomfortable for both parties, it can be done gracefully.

You then might add a short story of a circumstance where you
had to fire someone. Basically, you should communicate that it
was unfortunate, but it had to be done and you did it in a very
graceful manner.

Q. What kind of people have you hired and what do you look for in those people?

I have been fortunate to have available to me wonderful people whom I have added to my teams in the past. I look for committed, passionate performers. Fortunately, I can and have been able to attract them and, just as importantly, keep them!

Q. In your present or last jobs were there any problems that you discovered that had been previously overlooked? How did you deal with them?

When I came into my job, the department really didn't want to recognize the problem we had with inventory and delivery. We had a supply-chain software module that no one was using. It cost us nothing but a little time to implement and now everyone knows where everything is in the product delivery cycle.

Q. Describe a major project that you have worked on and how it contributed to the overall good of your employer?

If you have been involved in doing a major project, the perfect phrase would be to simply describe that project in relative detail.

I have been involved in two major long-term, five-year projects . . .

This is a place to tell a short story of your and your team's success.

Q. Have you ever been involved in long-range planning?

I chaired a committee for a long-range building (or product launch or company reorganization or . . .).

Don't claim that you were involved in long-range planning unless you really were, because you may very well be asked about your contribution. Your credibility will be questioned if you can't speak about what you did.

Q. Give me an example of your past job experience that highlights your ability to build action plans or create programs that support management's strategic goals and direction. (You need to have three or four stories that could be used interchangeably with questions like this. If in a previous answer you tell a story that could be an answer to this question, you don't want to tell the same story.)

My department was downsized and our workload was doubled. Rather than react to whatever project came our way, I convinced the team that we should outline a process . . . a more efficient process than simply reacting.

It's working. We are getting more done with fewer folks, and the rest of the company knows they can't just come to us and say, "Hey, we need this right now!" We aren't just reacting.

Q. What were the most important/difficult decisions that you made in your present job, last job, or even your job before that? (If you have to think about the answer to this question for more than a few moments, you appear as somebody who doesn't know what they're doing. It's best to have at least two or three ideas about what the most important or difficult decision was in all of the jobs that you have had.)

In the last two jobs I had to lay off 35 percent and 25 percent of my staff, respectively, in each position. It was difficult to decide who would stay and who would go. I did it with as much compassion and decisiveness as possible. It was hard, but it worked out very smoothly.

Q. What are one or two things you wished you had accomplished in your present or last job and the job before that?

The economics of the company were such that we had to shut down the development of two very good programs (or products and so on) *because the return on investment* (ROI) *was too far in the future.*

Q. Why have you not been promoted sooner? If you're so good, why haven't you been promoted? (Don't let a question like this get under your skin.)

The organization I am with has a bottleneck of very tenured people available for the few promotions when they come up. That is one of the reasons that I'm interviewing with you.

Q. You really don't have as much experience as we would like, why should we hire you?

With every job I've ever had, I never went into the job having all of the experience that the employers wanted. In fact, I went into three of them where I was hired simply because I had more potential than any other candidate.

As you can see, I was successful in every position.

QUESTIONS ON YOUR WORK ETHIC

Employers want to know what kind of person they're hiring. The interviewer will often ask questions to try to get a sense of your attitude toward your work. Your personal work ethic may include being reliable, having initiative, and pursuing new skills.

Q. What kind of job are you looking for?

I'm looking for a position that is going to help make a company better and challenge me based on my experience and background. I've had that in every job before.

Q. What motivates you?

I'm intrinsically motivated to live up to my potential by challenging myself to do the best I can every day.

Q. How do you define success?

When I contribute to a successful organization, I am successful. We both grow.

　　or

Success is the progressive realization of a worthy goal for both the company I work for and myself.

Remember. People love stories, and they remember them long after they remember most everything else, so tell a story that shows a time you contributed to a successful organization.

Q. Are you a good employee (or manager or engineer or accountant or salesperson or administrative support person or . . .)? How do you know?

I really love what I do. I am very good at it because I get a lot of positive feedback for the job that I do. My performance reviews and salary reviews have always been excellent. My track record reflects my success.

Q. What made you choose to become a_____?

Fortunately, I have a great gift for communicating with people (or "for numbers" or "for java development" or "for financial concepts"), *and I have honed that skill for a number of years. It has served me well and been a tremendous advantage for the people I have worked for.*

Q. How do you approach doing things that you really don't like to do?

Well, attitude is everything. I have found that no matter how much I don't like any particular aspect of my job, if I take the right attitude toward it, I've been very successful.

I try to break the particular job down into smaller steps and accomplish them one at a time. I find that, along with my attitude, to be the major reasons I'm successful in taking on parts of my job that I really don't like.

Q. Have you ever failed in a job?

I'm like a ballplayer who never really lost . . . he just ran out of time. Even the very few things that I look back on and others might see as failures, I really see as setbacks. But even when something didn't work out, I've learned from it.

Q. When faced with a difficult business decision, what do you do? (Make sure you communicate that you do go through a number of processes that communicate wisdom.)

Experience has taught me to think long and hard about the decisions I make. I think on paper by writing out all of the issues, then seeing how they appear to me over a period of time.

I seek the opinions of others who are both close to the situation as well as removed from it. I have two or three mentors whom I have developed over the years whose opinions I respect, and I seek their counsel.

When I have exhausted all of the processes that I might go through, I then follow my gut instinct. Once I have made the decision, I become committed to it 110 percent and throw myself behind it. Unless there is a drastic change in the facts, I am unwavering about the decision.

Q. How do you keep updated and informed in a professional sense?

I subscribe to two professional publications: _____ and _____. I'm an avid reader and always trying to hone my skills. Lately, I have been reading _____ by _____, and have found it very interesting.

Q. What is the most recent business lesson you have learned and how did you learn it?

I try to be a lifelong learner. Recently, I learned _____ _____.

Be ready with a recent lesson, like "how quickly the market can change." Tell a story to reinforce your response.

Q. Can you work overtime or on weekends?

I'll do whatever it takes to get the work done. I have found over my career that since I am a diligent worker, focused on the task at hand, and avoid wasting time with unproductive cohorts, I get more work done in a lot less time than most.

I'll work evenings and weekends if I have to, but that hasn't been necessary in the past.

Q. How many hours in your previous jobs did you have to work each week to get the job done? (Don't fall prey to this loaded question.)

Gee whiz, I'm not on a clock. I really don't know.

If you had a job where you were paid overtime, the hiring authority may be concerned about having to pay a lot of overtime. So, in a situation like this, you would answer by saying:

I was always very careful to be sure that I didn't work overtime unless I absolutely had to. I'm a fast worker and usually get my work done in the allotted time. Of course, my references would substantiate this.

Q. Can you relocate either now or in the future?

I will do anything that is good for my company and my career. Relocation would certainly be included.

Q. What are some of the things in your last job that you didn't like?

I was frustrated because most everybody was so negative about the poor situation of the company. It's true that the company was eventually sold, but the negativity was hard to deal with on an everyday basis.

Whatever you didn't like, make it a values thing or something you could do nothing about.

Q. What was the last thing you disagreed with your company about?

I really can't recall anything of any importance that I minded or disagreed with my company on. If there was something, whatever it might have been, I certainly don't remember.

Q. In what areas could your boss do a better job?

I have a lot of respect for my present boss. He (or she) *does his* (her) *job extremely well. There might be some little things that he* (she) *might be able to do a little better because of experience, but they must be minor.*

Whatever you say, don't criticize your boss, no matter what you think of him (or her).

Q. How well did you feel your boss rated your performance?

All of the supervisors or bosses I've had have given me good reviews.

If you have copies of any of these, either with you or that you can send to the interviewing authority, doing so would reinforce your claim.

Q. How did your boss or previous bosses get the best out of you? (This is a little bit of a trick question. Just be ready for a question like this and realize that there is a simple answer.)

By telling me exactly what the objectives are and then leaving me alone. My motivation is intrinsic.

Q. Highlight your experience in dealing with interpersonal conflict and disagreements by recalling a difficult situation that you were involved in. (Again, you need to have a story.)

One of my peers was promoted over me to become my boss. We never got along very well. It has been interesting. I have realized that I shouldn't compete with him. I sat down with him right when he first got promoted, and we came to an agreement of our mutual expectations. We aren't the best of friends, but we get along in our environment.

Q. Give me an example of when you were refused or told "no" by your company or supervisors.

Two years ago, I asked for a software upgrade from management. I asked in a very gracious way and was told "no" in a very gracious way, because of budget constraints.

I presented my case again every six months with a demonstration in long-term savings the company would realize. Three months ago, I was given the budget to do the upgrade. I was persistent, but nice.

Q. What is the most recent skill you have learned?

I've recently taken a course on negotiation as well as an online course with one of my company's proprietary IT applications.

Show that you are honing your skills all of the time.

Q. What is the most important professional lesson that you have learned from the jobs that you have had?

To be ready for the unexpected . . . unexpected consequences . . . unexpected resignations . . . people being people. Since we are going to make mistakes, be prepared. Making the mistakes isn't the issue; it is knowing how to react to the mistakes, minimize the damage, and rectify them quickly.

Q. If you could start your career over again, what would you do differently? (Answer this question very carefully.)

Looking back, I would have found mentors in the companies I worked for a little faster. I realize now that they can make your life a whole lot easier. I should've done it sooner.

Q. Do you want to move into management?

I do believe I have management potential, but I know that good leaders are also good followers. If I prove myself in my role, if there are opportunities to advance, I'm sure that I will be considered. I will try to do those jobs equally well. If I do the task at hand, future positions will take care of themselves.

QUESTIONS ABOUT YOUR WORK STYLE

You should be prepared to answer a variety of questions about your preferred work style. Above all, your answers should show that you are flexible.

Q. What would be your ideal work group?

I've worked in both large groups as well as small groups. Either one can be ideal.

Q. How would you define a "good-fit" work environment?

Where people respect each other and support each other's work.

Q. Do you work well with other people?

Absolutely. In fact, I'm often told how well I work in groups.

Have a story ready to demonstrate this point.

Q. Do you prefer to work alone or with other people?

Either way works well. I'm effective with either situation.

Q. Do you require lots of supervision?

Not at all. My references can attest to that.

Q. Do you communicate best with written or oral communications?

I seem to do well with either one.

Q. Are you creative?

Yes. I came up with a very unique solution to the _____ problem in my present position.

Simply cite one or two instances where you were creative. Keep all stories short and to the point.

Q. What are the things that you find most difficult to do?
(The answer here has to center around something you would not be expected to know well. For instance, if you are an accountant or an engineer in an organization, you would use the answer that follows.)

The most difficult challenge I have is to operate in a sales function.

If you are a salesperson, then you would say:

The most difficult challenge I have is operating in an accounting or technical function.

This seems rather obvious, but the answer is very safe.

Q. And how did you deal with those tasks?

I found someone in that department whose task was difficult for me to understand (define the department—accounting, engineering, sales, and so on) *and asked for their help.*

I often solicit the administrative people in those depart-
ments. Those people sometimes aren't given enough appre-
ciation for what they do and when someone from a different
department asks for their help, they are generally more than
happy to oblige.

Q. Has there ever been a situation where your work was crit-
icized?

There have been situations where I learned from the mistakes
I made in some of the work I did. I take criticism well and have
learned something from every time I've experienced it.

Q. What do you look for in a job?

I'd like the work to be challenging. I enjoy being challenged
every day. By being challenged, I'm going to grow personally
and professionally. If that happens, everything else takes
care of itself.

Q. Do you prefer to delegate or be a hands-on employee?

I feel comfortable in delegating those things that should be
delegated and personally doing the things that I do best. I
know that, when work is delegated, not everyone is going to
do the job just exactly the way I would. But I'm comfortable
with that.

Q. Describe a situation where you had to make a seat-of-
the-pants decision, without a company policy as a model.
(Think about two or three situations where you made off-the-
cuff decisions and how they wound up being very good decisions. You can tie these decisions to a working philosophy of

integrity, character, and a "do-the-right-thing" approach if you really want to look good.)

We made a big mistake with one of our customers. It wasn't really our fault . . . it was the fault of one of our subcontractors, but that didn't really matter. Rather than take it up with the rest of our company, I took full responsibility for our organization, right then. The customer was so surprised that he started asking on behalf of himself and his firm, "What can all of us do about it?"

Q. For what have you been most frequently criticized? (This is like the question about your biggest weakness. Think of something that could be positive or negative.)

Sometimes my expectations of people are greater than their capabilities. I work very hard, and I often expect others to do the same. When they don't, I question it. I have to remember that not everyone works that hard.

Q. Tell me about a time when you faced resistance or rejection to your ideas or actions. What did you do?

We had a project to do. I thought we could get it done in four weeks, if everyone pitched in and focused. People thought I was crazy. The resistance came because people would have to work harder and longer to get it done on time. I overestimated our ability to complete it on time. I was off by two weeks. But we got it done.

Q. We sometimes run into a person who makes unreasonable demands of us. Tell me about a time when this happened to you. (Once again, be ready with a story.)

I worked for a lady like that in my last job. I found that if I simply listened to her demands without reacting at the moment, then came back to her later with logical reasons about what she should expect, I managed to set expectations and get her demands to be more reasonable. The key was to not overreact when the demand was made. I calmed the waters.

Q. Describe a situation where you had worked with a very difficult person. How did you handle it?

He/she was difficult to work with/for, but I found a way and learned so much from them. I learned that their comments and style weren't personal and I didn't take them personally. It turned out to be a great learning experience, even though it was painful at times.

Q. Describe a situation where you had to make a quick decision in your last job. How do you make it?

I follow my gut based on some tremendous learning experiences I've had . . . both good and bad. For instance, I quickly reprimanded an employee who was difficult and uncooperative. I reprimanded her a number of times, so when I needed to fire her, we had plenty of documentation.

Q. How many levels of management have you had to communicate with?

In the smaller firms I have worked for, I communicated often with the CEO, even the board. In the larger firms, it was usually two levels up.

Q. Tell me about an experience that illustrates your preference between being proactive in speaking to and maintaining contact with others and waiting for others to speak first or contact you.

I knew our group's budget was going to be cut. I didn't know by how much, but I knew it was going to be cut. Instead of waiting until it came out and having to deliver the bad news to people and hear moaning and groaning, I prepared everyone beforehand by asking them to think about how they would proactively trim their budget before it was dictated to them. They felt more in control of their own destiny, and the cuts weren't as bad as we thought they would be. People were relieved, even proud of themselves, for being prepared.

Q. How have you shown resilience in the face of . . . ?

CONFLICT:

I stay calm . . . don't react to the emotion of the moment. I go away, take a deep breath, relax, and think.

FRUSTRATING CIRCUMSTANCES:

I try to remember, "This too will pass." We have been frustrated before and come out OK.

CONSTRAINTS:

I think about possibilities, see the glass as half full not half empty, and look for the positive.

RAPIDLY CHANGING CIRCUMSTANCES:

I think fast . . . think about possibilities . . . this could change again at any time.

SHIFTING PRIORITIES:

I'm really good at being ready for change.

ADVERSITY:

I remember the quote from Nietzsche: "What doesn't kill me makes me stronger."

MULTIPLE DEMANDS UPON TIME AND OTHER RESOURCES:

I prioritize, prioritize, and prioritize!

Q. Do you know when to lead and when to follow?

Good leaders are always good followers. I really try to do both.

Q. Can you identify the critical needs in a situation, deal with them, and put the others on the back burner?

Absolutely.

QUESTIONS ABOUT THE JOB ITSELF

Hiring authorities want to find out what you know about the job you're applying for. Are you simply responding to a job posting or do you really have interest in the job and the company?

Q. What do you know about the position you are applying for?

I know your organization is the kind that I would like to join, and from what I understand, my skills fit best in this position. Can you enlighten me as to exactly what this position entails?

This answer gets the interviewer to tell you more about the position.

Q. What makes you think you can handle this position?

In my last two jobs, I inherited a disaster. I've always been able to deal with very difficult situations.

Have one or two stories ready to back this statement up.

Q. The job for which you are interviewing requires you to wear a lot of different hats. You have never done some of these functions. How do we know that you are going to be able to do them?

Even though my primary functions were _____ and _____, in most of my positions I have successfully handled several different roles.

Then provide examples of where you performed a number of diverse activities.

Q. How do we know that you will be successful at this job?

I've been successful before; therefore, I know I will be successful again.

If you have to back up your statement, you can do it with success stories.

Q. What can you contribute most to our organization?

Over and above my excellent professional performance, as I've documented in previous positions, I work harder and am more committed to work than most employees. Next to my relationship with my family comes my work.

Q. What do you think makes the position you are interviewing for different from the jobs you've had or the other positions you are interviewing for? (Make sure that you communicate very positive reasons as to why the job you are interviewing for would be a better fit than the one you had in the past.)

The job here would be a great challenge. The best part is that the people here are really good. You all have done a great job in collecting the right folks.

Q. You seem overqualified for this job. You did this kind of thing a number of years ago. Why would you consider doing it again?

I've found that very few people are overqualified if they un-
derstand the challenge that the particular job would entail.
Some of the most challenging things that I've done and the
most gratifying were when I did this kind of thing at XYZ
Corporation.

This question comes from the interviewer's fear that, if you take the job, you will stay for a short time. You must reassure him that this isn't the case. My long-time friend and Grande Dame of all things career, Joyce Lain Kennedy (America's original careers columnist and author of twenty-three books on career development and management), suggests that "overqualified is usually code for one of five perceptions—too many years' experience, too much education, too highly paid, too rigid with demands, or too rusted with obsolete skills." She goes on to say, "Why go down with a one-word knockout punch? Come back with a strong response—or even a preemptive strike to clear the air."

I wouldn't accept the job if I thought I wouldn't be in it for
a very long period of time. I wouldn't do that to you or to
myself. The challenge in a job is what an employee makes it.
*   I know exactly what I'm getting into. You'll notice that*
I've been on average five (six, seven, eight) *years on the*
last few jobs that I've had, and I would expect to be on
this one for as long as it's here.

Q. With your experience and background, I don't think you
are capable of doing this job. What do you think?

The people I have worked for in the last two jobs had the
same concern before they hired me. I am an overachiever and

have always been able to perform well beyond my apparent capabilities.

Then tell a relevant story.

Q. How does our position compare with the other opportunities for which you are currently interviewing? (If you are considering other opportunities—and only if you are—use the powerful phrase that follows.)

Taking into consideration everything I know about the other opportunities I am interviewing for, the position here with you seems to be a little bit of a better match.

Just be sure that you have good reasons for saying that.

Q. If you could, what would you change about the position you're interviewing for?

Based on most everything I know, it seems that what you are asking for in the function of the position is reasonable. I really don't know enough about the position to know what might or should be changed.

Q. What do you like most about this position? And what do you like least about this position?

I'm very anxious to take on the responsibility of this job. _____ and _____ about the job are most exhilarating. I don't really think that there's anything about the job that I've heard so far that I'm going to dislike. I'm sure there are going to be some things that I will like more than others, but that's to be expected in any job.

Q. Why should I hire you?

Because I can do the job, I'm a hard worker, people like me, I'm not a great risk, and I'm sure we can come to an agreement about money.

Q. If you were offered this job, how long will it take you to decide?

If I were offered the job, I should be able let you know within a day or, at the most, two.

Q. How long would you expect to be at this position if you got it?

Every time I have left any situation, it has been primarily because I was really limited. I am very patient and have explored every opportunity to the maximum. There was no personal growth in the situations, even after I gave it time. As long as I am growing personally, intellectually, and professionally, I am committed to staying as long as I can. I hate changing jobs and companies.

QUESTIONS ABOUT THE COMPANY

Employers need to know that you have some knowledge about their business. They will ask questions to determine how much you know about the company itself and what they do.

Q. What do you know about our business?

From my research, I know that _____ (for example, you are a leader in _____, you all are new to _____, or the firm is growing rapidly).

Communicate short, direct bits of information about their company and their business.

Q. What is our business's biggest challenge or problem?

From my research I know _____. *Is that correct?*

Again, it isn't hard to get this information.

Q. What trends do you see in our profession or industry?

My research and experience says _____.

Be sure you have a good business observation.

Q. What do you know about our competition?

My research tells me that they really respect you. They say you are really a formidable competitor.

Q. What do you know about our company?

My research has revealed three things. First, _____. *Second,* _____. *Third,* _____.

These points should be really good insights into the company. By the way, stating "first," "second," and "third" followed by concise points makes a great impression of precise thinking.

Q. Why did you apply to our company? (Here's a chance to demonstrate the research you've done on the company and to communicate your specific skills by using the following powerful phrase.)

You and your firm are leaders in the business (specify business, for example, accounting, finance, engineering, design). *I have been a very hard-working and successful* _____ (accountant, financial manager, engineer, designer). *I want to be associated with winners.*

Q. If you could choose any organization to work for, where would you go?

All of the organizations that I am talking to are quality firms with quality people just like this one. All of the positions that I am interviewing for have their strengths and weaknesses. A job is pretty much what you make it once you show up and start working. I see the opportunity to work here in your firm as one of the best opportunities available to me.

Q. How long do you think it will take for you to make a meaningful contribution to our organization?

In my present job, I began to make a significant contribution almost immediately. The nature of the work was such that I could go right in and immediately have an impact. It was really fun.

In the job before that, because of the nature of what the company did, it took me five or six months to have a significant impact.

All the people that I have ever worked with have always said that I'm a quick study and pick things up very quickly.

Q. What reservations might you have about working here?

None that I know of. No job or company is perfect, and I'm sure that you have your positives and negatives just like any other company.

QUESTIONS FOR MANAGEMENT POSITIONS

Although you will have to answer many of the same questions as those above when you're applying for a management position, there will be certain questions specific to your management experience.

Q. What is your management style?

I don't know if I can give my management style a particular title or description. I do know that in the past I've created an environment where people feel like we're all in this together. I've been very successful in getting people to do more than they normally would in many circumstances.

If you label yourself as one kind of management style as opposed to another, you might describe yourself differently than the hiring authority who is interviewing you. By not labeling yourself, but providing examples of your management or leadership style, as well as providing a story demonstrating your style, you play it safe.

Q. How would you define your job as a manager?

My job as a manager is to reach the goals and objectives of the company by hiring and motivating the right kinds of people.

Q. What type of turnover have you had as a manager?

Relative to my profession, I had very little turnover in my management positions. Fortunately, I hired good people and helped them stay motivated.

Q. How do you motivate your subordinates?

I always try to communicate a "we-are-all-in-this-together" attitude. When I've done that, folks get motivated. It may be a cliché, but I communicate there is no "I" in "team."

Q. Give us an example of how you got your staff to support an unpopular decision.

I had to cut our budget by $80,000. So, I gave my team a choice: We could all, including me, take a 10 percent pay cut for the year, or I'd have to lay off at least one, if not two people. Everyone—to a person—accepted the pay cut.

This kind of question won't come up often, but be ready for it and have a good story.

Q. What special problems do you have with the day-to-day management of your staff? (If the situation is applicable, the following answer would be an example of a perfect phrase.)

My team is dispersed all over the country, and I have to coordinate everyone's activities. Time zones and different people's schedules are a challenge.

Q. Do you have budgetary responsibility? How large was your budget? Did you have any problems staying within budget?

I had a budget of $_____ and I was always within it.

Q. Explain your hiring procedure.

Hiring is one of the most important things I have done. I've always been very fortunate in being able to discover really good people. I have a very specific multistep process of hiring, which has kept me from making as many mistakes as most. I still operate on what I've learned from one of my mentors: "Hire slowly, fire quickly."

Q. Describe the biggest mistake you made in hiring.

I hired a candidate one time who was almost too perfect. Looking back on it, there was a reason for that . . . the candidate who was hired was a big liar and he was really good at it. I should have recognized that he was too good to be true. I really learned from the mistake.

Q. Tell me about a situation where you were disappointed in your own performance.

There have been a few times when I have overestimated my team's ability to perform. I wasn't as disappointed in the performance as I was disappointed in my overestimation. I certainly learned from it

Q. Give me an example of a new or innovative idea that you came up with or implemented.

*I came up with a way of reorganizing our invoicing that has
reduced our accounts receivable time by thirty-five days.*

**Q. Have you ever had to carry out unpopular policies or deci-
sions?**

*Two years ago, I had to explain to my staff how everybody
was being asked to take a 15 percent reduction in salary to
save everyone's job. Not one of my subordinates quit. They
didn't even complain.*

Q. What are people's greatest misperceptions about you?
(Think for a moment and pause.)

*Well, sometimes it may appear that I take things too seriously
and come across as not having a sense of humor.*
     or
*I sometimes might appear to be a workaholic and have high
expectations of others.*

**Q. Tell me about a time when you had to get your hands dirty
by doing a job that was one or two steps below you.**

*Just last week two people in our accounting department
were out for three days. It was kind of fun to get back into
the trenches and do invoicing as well as collection calls.*

Q. As a manager, how have you promoted diversity?

*I've been able to hire a diverse group of great people. I make
sure to spread the responsibility equally.*

Q. How much do you know about the duties or responsibilities of the managers two levels below you?

I've been fortunate to always be able to actually take on the duties and responsibilities of the subordinates that I've had. I have functioned in most of their jobs before . . . either in my present company or companies I've worked for previously. They recognize that I understand every aspect of their jobs.

Q. You have moved up in the management ladder rapidly, but it seems like you've leveled off. Why?

There are a lot of very good people and managers in the company that I am presently with. They've been there for quite some time. Their seniority and quality is hard to beat. That is one of the major reasons that I am looking to change.

On top of that, my personal growth and expansion is limited there. So, when I add these two factors up, it is best that I find a new job for both the company and me.

If I'm not growing and reaching my potential, I'm not going to be able to maximize my contribution. It's mutually best for both of us that I leave.

Q. How have you dealt with disgruntled employees or subordinates?

I've been fortunate enough to establish personal policies and procedures so that most all of my subordinates have known where I stand on certain issues. I have found that being consistent, even about things that everyone may not agree with, has been the first and best line of defense.

I have found that 90 percent of the time, simply listening to people, especially when they need to vent, dissipates most issues. In checking my references, you will find that I have always managed people that way. I have found that even the most disgruntled subordinate respects fairness.

Q. How often have you fired someone?

Fortunately, even when I've had to fire anyone, I have made it good for both of us. I document the reasons so it is very objective. I want to be sure it never comes across as capricious or reactionary. I have tried to create an atmosphere and environment where people who aren't going to make it or don't fit in leave before I have to fire them.

Q. Have you ever doubted your decision about firing someone?

If there are doubts to begin with, I have tried to work the situation out with the person before I have had to fire them. But once I have let them go, I can't afford to look back and doubt the decision. If it comes to the point where I have to let someone go, I'm sure of myself.

BE PREPARED

The answers to "can-you-do-the-job?" questions need to communicate confidence. You should be ready for questions you don't think about every day. Your work style, for example, isn't something that you articulate on a daily basis. But in the interviewing situation, the answer must roll off your tongue as though you recite it all the time.

The "can-you-do-the-job?" questions are probably the most taken for granted by candidates. They think they will have an easy time answering these questions. Don't take for granted that you will be able to give confident, competent answers. Prepare in advance for a variety of questions with powerful words and phrases such as those provided in this chapter. Have relevant stories ready to expand upon your answers. And above all else: Practice, practice, practice!

5 Powerful Phrases That Show You Will Be a Good Fit

Based on my experience, determining whether you will be a good fit in the company accounts for about 40 percent of the hiring decision. Of the four basic questions that need to be answered affirmatively (see Chapter 4), this carries the greatest weight. It comes down to whether or not the potential employer likes you. No matter how good your skills might be, no matter how much of a risk you may or may not be, and even if working the money out is a foregone conclusion, you will never get hired unless you are liked and the people interviewing you think you are a good fit.

Of the more than 110,000 face-to-face interviews I have personally arranged since 1973, I've never had a candidate hired who wasn't, at first, liked by the people doing the interviewing and hiring. This fact defies logic and common sense. With all of the business acumen and wisdom that companies and the people in them are purported to have, you'd think that the emotional aspects of liking someone would have a minimal impact.

But the truth is that hiring people is like buying products. People do it for emotional reasons and then justify the rest. I can't tell you the number of people I've placed over the years who were hired simply because they were liked by the hiring organization. I also can't tell you how many extremely qualified, excellent candidates weren't hired because the interviewing or hiring authority did not initially like them.

You can control whether you are liked by hiring authorities by showing them that you are a good fit. As a candidate, you can't control certain "cultural" fits like age, gender, religion, or schooling (for example, graduating from Ivy League schools). However, if you research your interviewing authorities and find out about their backgrounds, you can demonstrate something in common with them. By doing that you are further on your way to being "liked."

COMMONLY ASKED QUESTIONS TO SEE IF YOU ARE A GOOD FIT

These questions will be sprinkled throughout the interview. They are going to be personal as well as professional questions. Oftentimes, you could be insulted by them if you let yourself. (Some may actually be illegal.) But you can never let these or any other kinds of questions throw you off emotionally. You can't interview well when you are emotionally flustered.

What follows are some of the most frequent "Are you a good fit?"/"Do we like you?" questions and the most effective powerful phrases to use as answers.

Q. Are you a leader or follower?

Well, in certain situations I am a leader and in certain situations I am a follower. I can be both.

Reinforce this answer with stories, if possible.

Q. What do people like most about you?

People seem to appreciate that I am a team player (deal well in tense situations . . . volunteer to help . . . communicate well both up and down the chain of command).

Pick a phrase that relates to work. Don't just say something like, "I'm a good guy" or "I know a lot about sports."

Q. What do they like least? (Regarding what people like least about you, keep your answer light. Laugh and say something like the following example.)

I'm a lousy golfer (or a poor tennis player or I'm not good at telling jokes).

Q. What are your three greatest strengths? (Strengths should be easy for you to come up with. You should determine your answers well before you even start interviewing.)

I'm a very hard worker, determined and persistent.

Q. What are your three greatest weaknesses? (Weaknesses are always difficult, but make sure your "weaknesses" can also be strengths.)

Well, I'm often impatient with myself.
    or
I often expect the same passion and commitment from the others that I tend to have.

I have known people to say just plain stupid things like, "Well, to be honest, I talk too much" . . . "I'm late a lot" . . . "I seem to have bad luck in jobs and get fired" . . . "I have bad luck with women and jobs" . . . "I get bored easily." Don't say anything remotely like that!

Q. What are your hobbies? Outside interests? Books you've read recently? (Make your hobbies "safe" and related to the business world. Don't talk about anything controversial like church groups or political groups unless you know the interviewing authority feels the same way you do. Talk about hobbies like golf, tennis, running, cycling, and so on.)

My woodworking hobby allows me to work with my hands. When my mind is relaxing while doing it, I often think of business solutions.

When asked about books you've been reading, make sure you are reading some kind of business-oriented book and mention it. This kind of question is easy to prepare for and you can give the same answer to everyone.

I'm rereading Great by Choice *by Jim Collins. Every time I read it I come up with some new ideas.*

Q. What do you like and dislike about your present boss?

I really like him (or her) *as a person and have learned a lot from him* (or her).

Do not say anything negative about your current boss.

Q. How do you handle criticism?

I really do appreciate constructive criticism; I think feedback is the breakfast of champions. I am my own worst critic, but I really like hearing what other people think.

Q. Rate yourself on the scale of one to ten.

Well, my spouse thinks I'm a ten . . . sometimes! However, when I rate myself, I am an eight or nine in some things and a six or seven in others. But you will find I do my dead-level best to do well in everything I do.

Q. How would others at your present or previous jobs rate you on a scale of one to ten?

I think some of them would rate me as an eight or nine in some of the things I do and six or seven in other things I do. But they do know that I try to do my best in everything I do.

Q. Do you ever lie? (This is a catch-22 question.)

If I'm invited to a social occasion that I really don't want to go to, I will say that I have other plans. I guess, technically, that's a lie, but I see no sense in hurting other people's feelings by telling them that I don't wish to socialize with them.

If the interviewer probes deeper on this question, offer this phrase:

It is important to be truthful in all aspects of business. I think lying is basically wrong and should only be used in situations

as the last graceful alternative where the results are inconse-
quential.

Q. What are one or two things your present or previous co-workers dislike about you?

Nobody has ever outright told me anything about myself that they said they disliked. I sometimes get the feeling that my work ethic and my striving for perfection irritate some people.

I'm often very direct and to the point. I'm not sure everybody can handle that kind of honesty.

Q. What makes you mad?

There aren't very many things that make me mad, but I do get frustrated, especially with some of the things that my sixteen-year-old does (laugh).

I have found that getting mad or angry doesn't help solve the immediate problem. I don't think any of us perform well under the emotional stress of anger.

Q. How do you make your opinions known when you disagree with management or your boss?

If my opinions are sought out, I respectfully offer them. If they're not sought out, and it is not within my responsibility, I probably wouldn't offer my opinion.

If I felt strongly enough about the issue and thought it was important to voice my opinion, I would make a private appointment with the appropriate person to discuss my thoughts.

Q. If you knew then what you know now, how would you change your life or your career? (This is a really good question and you need to have a really good answer for it. You should mention things that might be obvious. For instance, if you have not completed your degree, you might say that, looking back on it, you would have finished your degree. If you have had a couple of very short-term jobs on your resume, you might say that if you knew then what you know now, you wouldn't have taken those jobs. After you mention the obvious things, use the following powerful phrase.)

The important thing, for me, is that I've learned from every mistake I've ever made and, fortunately, I haven't made the same mistake more than once. I know I will make others, but I'm going to make the best of what I learn from them, too. It would be nice if the lessons hadn't been so painful.

Don't ever say that you "wouldn't change a thing" because, even it if this is true, not many people will believe you.

Q. What is your definition of success? Of failure? (These are loaded questions that have no absolutely correct answer.)

Success for me is the constant pursuit of a worthy goal where I am personally growing and economically providing for myself and my family.

The only definition of failure, for me, would be when people quit trying and give up. Failure is not an option for me, nor should it be for anyone else.

Q. What makes you better than any other candidate I can hire?

On paper, I may not be better than anyone else. But I am a very hard worker, and I am determined to be successful. In the final analysis, I have more passion and commitment to the job than most people do.

So, with me, you get passion, commitment, and determination far above what you'd probably get in most anybody else.

Q. I'm sure that there were some policies in your previous companies that you didn't agree with. How did you handle those?

There might have been some minor policies and procedures that I didn't agree with, but, for the most part, the policies and procedures were for the good of the company and everybody in it.

Don't ever bad-mouth previous employers or their policies!

Q. What kind of people do you hang out with? (Be a little careful with this question. Some interviewing authorities may be trying to ask you about church groups, political organizations, ethnic groups, and so forth.)

I have a diverse group of friends who are all very interesting.

If you were asked about hobbies and you mentioned golf or tennis, you might say that you hang out with people like that.

Q. How would you describe your personality?

I'm pretty even-keeled. I can get excited about stuff but take it all in stride. I try not to let the highs be too high and the lows be too low.

Q. We're a very aggressive organization here. You seem to be a fairly laid-back, rather quiet person. How do you get along with aggressive folks?

When people get to know me, they don't think that I am really all that quiet. I am intensely interested in the opportunity with your company, so I'm trying to listen hard to what you're saying.

I've always been able to get along with just about every kind of person and personality.

Q. How did you feel the last time you joined a new company and a new group of people? How long did it take you to integrate with them personally?

It didn't take me long to get to know and integrate well with the people with whom I worked. I try to start out asking people about themselves—everybody's favorite subject—and that gets me accepted pretty fast.

Q. How do you deal with people who you don't like and who don't like you in the workplace?

I try to respect all of the people whom I encounter; even the people I don't particularly like or who don't seem to respect me. I deal with everybody on a professional level and try to keep personal relationships at work to a minimum.

I have to appreciate everyone, but I don't necessarily have to like them.

Q. Describe a very difficult person that you had to work with and how you handled the situation? (You can begin to an-

swer this question in a light-hearted way by smiling and saying, "My teenage daughter at times . . ." but then add something
powerful.)

*Seriously, I've never really had a problem with difficult peo-
ple even if they did not respect me personally. I have found
the best way to deal with difficult people, as with all other
people in the workplace, is to perform so well that my work
speaks for me, and what people think of me personally
doesn't really matter.*

**Q. Have you ever gotten personally involved or socially close
to anyone at your work?**

*I keep my personal life and business life separate. I have seen
situations where people have become personally involved
when they work together, and it usually leads to nothing but
a disaster. It just plain isn't smart.*

**Q. On a personal level what would your previous boss or
present boss say about you?**

*I've always got along very well with my bosses. I think that
everyone I've ever worked for both directly and indirectly
thought highly of me. But beyond social engagements like
dinners or golf games, I've always tried to keep our relationships on a business level.*

Q. We play a lot of poker (or, for example, golf, tennis, or bowl-
ing) **around here. Are you any good at it?** (Even if you are a
scratch golfer, never admit to being really good at any social
game or endeavor. You set yourself up as "someone to beat."
The phrase to use should be what follows.)

I do enjoy a competitive game of poker and seem to be able to hold my own.

Q. What was it like for you growing up? (The best answer is to describe your growing up as a "great" experience.)

Growing up was a great experience. My family instilled excellent values and a strong work ethic. I'm very fortunate.

If, in growing up, you had to overcome personal or family challenges, and they communicate a positive attitude or strong work ethic, certainly you can describe the experience. But be careful what you say!

Q. Have you ever had to overcome any personal hardships? (Whatever you'd do, do not describe your terrible, acrimonious divorces; your run-ins with the law; your DWIs; your being thrown out of your house by your spouse; your three bankruptcies; or anything that communicates poor judgment.)

We didn't grow up with a lot of money. Since I was 18, I have been pretty much on my own. I put myself through college and graduate school. Looking back, what seemed to be hardships at the time were really blessings. I learned from every one of them.

Q. If you were to invite three famous people to dinner, whom would you invite? (This is a dumb question, but if you are asked it, you pretty much have to answer it. Avoid politicians, religious figures, entertainers, or anybody else who could be considered remotely controversial. Sticking to business-oriented individuals, alive or dead, is safe.)

Jack Welch, Warren Buffett, and Bill Gates.

You could also pick people known for their business writing, such as:

Malcom Gladwell, Tom Peters, and Peter Drucker.

Q. If you were me, what question should I ask that you really don't want to answer? (This is also a dumb question, but it gets asked more than most people might think. The idea is to take you off your guard. Be ready! Keep your answer very light and almost funny.)

My golf handicap.

Q. Do you like me as a person?

Well, I don't know you very well at all. I think we have good chemistry. You are a very good interviewer.

Q. Describe a situation where you personally or professionally failed? (Watch out for this trap. Be ready for this question and answer it with a "safe" story—something like not making your high-school or college basketball team, getting a B in a very difficult class, or not getting a promotion that you felt you deserved will work.)

I failed to get into any of the three Ivy League colleges I applied to. I put a tremendous amount of effort in getting accepted to those schools. It was disappointing. I ended up going to the state school and it turned out to be a wonderful experience. I wouldn't trade it for the world.

If you describe a professional failure, make sure you don't blame other people. Take responsibility in the right way. Say something like:

We misjudged the market.
   or
We didn't see the recession coming.

Never blame others for your mistakes, even if they were part of it. You don't want to be perceived as a finger-pointer.

Q. How do you rank yourself personally and professionally among your peers? (You don't want to be too boastful or too humble in answering this question.)

I have been fortunate to work with a very successful, hard-driving organization where the performance bar is set pretty high. It is a great challenge to work with such a high-caliber group. Sometimes I outperform most everyone, and sometimes I am outperformed.

The great thing is that regardless of my rank, I am pressed to perform my best every time. Whether I come in first, second, or third isn't as important as the fact that I grow personally every day.

Q. Do you have personal and professional goals?

I have personal and professional goals. I write them at the beginning of every year, review them daily, and assess them quarterly. I believe everyone has to have goals.

Q. Who is your greatest personal mentor? (One has to be careful here. You need to be careful. Saying something like, "Jesus

Christ, my Lord and savior," might be the truth, but it is real risky to say. You're on much safer ground with examples like those that follow.)

My mother . . . my father . . . my older brother or sister . . . my high school football coach . . . my first boss.

Then give a short story about how this person was your mentor.

Q. What is the biggest personal mistake you have ever made? (This is a loaded question. If you say something like, "I married the wrong person and it turned out to be a disaster," you run a real risk. It is simply too emotionally charged and you never know how the hiring or interviewing authority is going to interpret the answer. So, it is best to play it safe and come up with something like making a personal investment that went badly, not finishing a degree, or taking a job that turned out to be a poor decision due to not doing enough due diligence.)

I invested in a company that went bust in the last recession. It cost me a lot of money.

Q. How did you get your last job?

I worked through a great recruiter who not only got me the interview, but helped me beat out nine other very qualified candidates.

Q. What do you do in your spare time? (Your answer to this minor question could wind up being a major mistake. If you say something like, "I work on my golf handicap every chance

I get," the hiring authority may fear that you are going to be playing golf when you are supposed to be making sales calls.)

Business is my avocation as well as my vocation. I read a lot of business books and attend lots of seminars on my own time.

Q. What you think about yourself is most important to us?
(If this question comes in the beginning of the interviewing process, then you want to sell the simple but important aspects that a company would want you to have as an employee.)

My commitment, passion, and hard work.

If you're deeper into the interviewing process and you have really done your homework, you should be aware of the most important attributes that the organization is looking for in any candidate.

I understand you all would like to get the company to $200 million. I have helped two organizations double their size in the last ten years. One went from $200 million to $400 million and another from $250 million to $500 million.
I know how to help get you where you want to go.

Q. Tell me about a business experience where you had to decide to either lead or to follow. What choice did you make and how did it turn out?

In my last position I took on responsibility for leading the conversion project because I had a hands-on knowledge of the accounting system and had worked with the SAP software before. Although there were others that had been with the firm longer, it was clear I could be the most logical choice.

The project was delivered three weeks earlier than we pro-jected.

or

Every good leader knows when to follow. When it's clear that a situation calls for me to listen to others, I go with the flow.

Q. Tell me about a time when you practiced diplomacy when communicating with another person or group. (Simply be ready for this question with a reasonable story.)

Last year, I had to disband one of the departments that I managed. We laid two people off and reassigned four others throughout the company. It was a purely economic decision, but politically very touchy.

We were so careful about the whole process, even with the people we laid off, that when we invited one of them to return to work after four weeks, he came back with no hard feelings.

Q. Tell me about the last time one of your subordinates made a big mistake. What did you do?

I understood exactly what the mistake was. When I reported it to my superiors, I explained that I was the one that was responsible. I didn't tell my superior that I should have been checking my subordinate's work, so he never knew who actually made the mistake. But it was my responsibility.

Q. What have you done to implement improvements in your work group organization? (Your answer to this question should be decisive and precise.)

I invited a productivity consultant into the organization and the whole department took his instructions. It required them to stay late an hour and a half one evening a week for eight weeks, but it was well worth it. Our productivity improved 15 percent.

Q. Sometimes we have to bring conflict out into the open and other times avoid it. Tell me about when you've had to make a choice like this.

Our customer service people were constantly angry at our outside salespeople because they claimed the salespeople were promising things we couldn't do, like with pricing and delivery times. I brought them together for 45-minute meetings every week to review the accounts. It promoted a "we-are-all-in-this-together" attitude. After the first rather tense meeting, everyone resolved the conflict and things have become a lot better.

Q. We all have to deal with power struggles or resolve win/ lose situations. Tell me about the last time you were involved in such a situation. (Depending on how the interview is going, you might laugh and say, "Well the last time was my spouse and I were deciding where to go to dinner. . . . I let him/her win." Then follow up with a serious work-related answer.)

My experience has been to create a situation where no one feels like they lose. The environment has to be "we are all in this together." When one loses, we all lose; when one wins, we all win.

Follow with an appropriate story.

Q. Describe to me how you make decisions. (If this question catches you off guard, you'll be dead in the water. Saying things like, "Well I just follow my gut" won't be a good answer.)

I sort out all the facts and write them out so I can see the pros and cons. I ask advice from people with experience and knowledge. Then I decide. It's important to make the right decision, of course, but I've learned that if I ever come to the conclusion that my decision was wrong, I need to admit it and change it quickly.

Q. Describe a time when an external customer tried to get something from you or your company that they didn't deserve, maybe not outright cheating, but close to it. How did you handle it and what did you do?

I had a situation where I knew the customer was being totally unreasonable. The customer's CEO was fond of yelling and screaming at people, getting them emotionally upset, and eventually getting his way. I didn't give in to that. I sent him an e-mail and made a reasonable offer to compromise. He kept trying to call me. He even called my boss and yelled at him. After a number of weeks, we agreed to settle.

Q. Describe a time when an internal customer tried your patience.

Our accounting department was consistently getting reports to us so late that our reports to the board were being thrown together at the last minute. Accounting people, in situations like this, aren't very flexible. So, I simply went to the departments that were giving the accounting department the information they needed and moved their deadline dates back one week. The accounting department was happy and so was everyone else.

Q. Priorities constantly change in our firm. Recurring challenges and limitations to resources push us really hard. Often it is hard to maintain a positive attitude, and the department gets emotionally down. Has this ever happened to you and how did you deal with it?

I try to look for the positive in every situation. That doesn't mean that I ignore reality, it just means I say to myself and the folks I work with, "There's a positive solution to this . . . what is it?" and say things like, "Two years from now we'll look upon this and laugh about how we solved the problem." This kind of positive attitude is very infectious and people buy into it.

Q. We all have times when we are very proud of what we've accomplished, and sometimes we don't receive the recognition we think we should. Tell me about a time that this has happened to you and how did you deal with it?

Getting external recognition isn't as important to me as my knowing that I have done a good job. I'm intrinsically motivated. I care more about living up to my own expectations than hearing praise from others.

Q. Describe a situation where you demonstrated a high level of commitment to an organization where you worked. (Be ready for a question like this. If you say something like, "I stayed late when I needed to . . . worked overtime when necessary . . . came in on the weekends when I had to," or something weak like that, you will lose points for a poor answer.)

Another department manager had a heart attack in the middle of chairing a major committee. I happened to be on the committee. Most everyone was at a loss as to what to do and how long it would take him to get back and so on. I volunteered to chair the group. Unfortunately, he never came back and took early retirement. But our committee accomplished its task.

Q. What have you done in the past that has demonstrated a high level of personal integrity?

My department miscalculated the costs on one of the proposals we made to a client. After we won the contract, we realized our mistake. I went to our CEO and explained the situation. He wasn't a happy camper! We decided that I would call the customer and explain what happened. The customer realized that we needed to make a profit in order to fulfill service after the project was completed. We compromised and wound up getting two more jobs from that organization.

Q. What was the last creative idea that you came up with that affected the group or company that you now work for? How did you come up with the idea? (You'd better have a good answer for this question. If you have to think about the answer for more than just a moment, you won't appear like you're telling the truth.)

When one of our major customers signed a multiyear contract with us, I came up with the idea to station one of our employees on-site with the client. This facilitated communications with the customer as well as made the customer feel important. The idea just seemed like a logical thing to do.

Q. What will your boss say when you resign? Will he or she be upset?

I'm sure my boss will be somewhat disappointed, but he (or she) has always been the kind of person who wants what's best for everyone in their organization. If finding a new job is best for my family and me, my boss might be unhappy about the situation for his and our company's sake, but he (or she) will be pleased for me.

Q. What will you miss most about your present job?

The people. It seems like every place I've ever worked, I've had the good fortune to work with wonderful people. But I'll bet there are wonderful people here in your organization also.

HOW THIS AFFECTS YOU

Most people think it's terribly unfair that being liked has as much to do with getting hired as it does. Hardly any hiring authority is going to admit how much it affects the hiring decision. While the first 20 percent of the hiring decision is based on your ability to do the job, being liked or considered a good fit with the rest of the company and the individuals in it is a major factor in getting hired.

In addition to the people who make judgments based on the interview, there's still going to be a personal compatibility assessment on the part of the hiring authority. People simply will not hire someone they don't like. (And you probably wouldn't go to work for someone you don't like. It works both ways.)

Now there will always be people who may not like you as much as they like others. That can't be helped, but, as a candidate, you need to be prepared for a personal evaluation. You have to be ready to be judged by your social skills as well as your professional skills.

I know it's hard to practice being liked. What's important is to be aware that being liked is a big part of getting hired. Once you realize that, you are better prepared to succeed in the process.

6 Powerful Phrases for Dealing with Problems in Your Background

These are going to be the most difficult questions you will be asked. They're going to encroach on your character, your judgment, and the quality of your decisions, both personally and professionally. Now, the truth is that everyone who has ever been hired is a risk. The real question embedded in this subject is, "What kind of risk are you?" And along with that, "Am I, as a hiring authority, willing to run the risk and put my reputation on the line with this person?"

A hiring authority is trying to *minimize* risk and *maximize* a return on investment. It's a trade-off. Hiring authorities want to minimize their risks, but get as many benefits as possible from hiring someone. The greater the risks you might present, the more they have to be offset by a greater reward. With every risk you present, you have to offset those risks with the benefits you can provide. The greater the benefits you can demonstrate, and the more risks you can mitigate, the better chance you have to be hired.

Candidates often don't recognize the risks that they present to a prospective employer. In fact, things you think are a positive might very well be a big liability. For instance, most people who have been the president of a company or owned their own firm think that these facts are great assets. I hear it all the time: "Wouldn't they want a candidate who knows how to run his own business?" The truth is they don't! These perceived assets are really liabilities. Most employers don't want to hire someone who may come in and try to run the show. So, being the president of a company or owning your own company is not an asset at all. They are risk factors.

Most candidates don't realize that hiring authorities are looking at as many reasons *not* to hire as they are to hire you. They perceive the glass to be half-empty more than they see the glass to be half-full. If you have had three jobs in three years, they are going to think that you are only going to be on their job for a year. If you were fired in your last position, they are going to think this means they may have to end up firing you. If you've been out of work for more than six months, they are going to wonder what's wrong with you.

You're going to have to meet these challenges head-on. Keep in mind that you cannot justify them. Saying to a prospective employer, "I know I've been out of work for two years, but so have a lot of other people. Don't you know that this is a lousy economy?" will not—I repeat, will not—help you as a candidate.

You will notice that one of the techniques I'm going to recommend using in some of the situations is what psychologists call "changing the base." It is turning a negative into a positive. It is using a powerful phrase to turn a risk into an asset. Many times it can be summed up with the phrase:

That is the very reason you should hire me!

For instance, if the hiring or interviewing authority expresses a concern about you having three jobs in three years, a powerful phrase would be:

That's the very reason that you should hire me; I can't afford to have another short stint on my résumé. Two of the last three firms that I worked for, unfortunately, have gone out of business. I'd still be there if they hadn't. As long as you will stay in business, I'll be the first one here every day and the last one to leave. I need to stay with you for many years.

Notice here that we turned a perceived negative into a positive. We changed the "base" to a positive. Let's get started. Once in a while, I'm going to offer you more than one phrase for certain critical, difficult questions.

COMMONLY ASKED QUESTIONS ON WHETHER YOU ARE A RISK

Q. Why do you want to leave where you are? . . . or . . . Why did you leave your last position? (Remember. Employers identify with other employers. Saying anything negative or disparaging about the company that you are presently with, or are leaving, is not going to do you well. Let me repeat: Saying anything negative about the people that you are working for or have worked for will be disastrous.)

I really love my job, I like the people I work with, and I appreciate everything the organization has done for me. However, the company is in the process of being sold (or under new management or has been contracting for the past few years and so on), *and I am personally stymied in my professional challenge and personal growth.*

Now that you've laid the groundwork, you want to explain your move in a way the hiring authority will understand. You're not being negative about your current (or previous) company; you're just looking for a better position.

> *I can stay in the position that I am in, but for the next several years I'm not going to be able to grow beyond the job I'm in now. Since my growth is limited, both personally and professionally, everything else, including my earnings, will stagnate. I owe it to myself and my family to seek a new opportunity where I can grow and be challenged beyond the position that I have now.*

You can also describe the job for which you're interviewing as an advancement over the job you have now and mention how much you will contribute to their company if they hire you.

> *This particular position that I'm interviewing for will give me the opportunity to_____, as well as really contribute to the growth of your organization. I'm just not able to do that where I am now. It isn't anybody's fault. It's the nature of what we do and the size of our organization.*

Q. You've stayed short periods of time in your last three jobs. What's wrong? (The obvious fear behind this question is that, if you are hired, you will only stay at that job for a short period of time.)

While you are correct that I've had three very short stints in my employment, there are two things that are very important. First of all, I don't like it better than anyone else; in fact, it has really concerned me. I made mistakes in taking a couple of those positions, and if knew then what I know now, I would never have done that.

Now you must turn the negative into a positive:

The fact that I've had three relatively short positions is one of the very reasons I can guarantee stability. I cannot afford another short stint at a job, so I am being very careful about the next job I take. Whoever hires me is going to get a passionate, committed employee for at least several years.

Then explain what a hard-working, committed employee they'll be getting if they hire you.

Even though the opportunities did not last very long, I worked hard while I was there. The references I have from those organizations will substantiate how hard I worked and how much I contributed.

It does not do any good at all to try to justify two or three short jobs that appear on your résumé. That is a road to disaster.

Q. You've been the president of a firm or the owner of your own firm. How do we know that you can work for someone else . . . or that you will take direction? (You'll first need to deflect the assumption that you won't be comfortable answering to someone else after running your own show.)

As president of an organization (or owner of a firm) *I answered to customers, employees, the government, the IRS, my attorneys, my CPAs, insurance companies, vendors . . . and very often, my spouse. We all answer to someone.*

Then explain how you recognize that the responsibility is on you to be a good employee.

I have never met a good leader who couldn't work within any organization, and be part of a team, as well as a good follower. In this opportunity, I may not lead the organization, but I still work for myself. My future earnings will be dependent upon how I perform. The only difference is that someone else will sign the paycheck.

Next, you must present the positive aspects you'll bring to the organization:

One great advantage in hiring me is that because I have been president of my own firm (or owned my own company), *I understand how hard it is to run a business. More than anyone else you will interview, I will treat your money like my money because I really understand how that works.*

Finish strong to allay the lingering fears of the hiring authority:

This all means that I'm going to work just as hard for you as I worked for myself. I take direction just as well as I give it, I follow just as well as lead, and I do what needs to be done. My ego is in check. I'm interested in the opportunity because I know I can do a good job for a very good company.

Q. You have been out of work for six months (or eight months or one year to two years or . . .). **What's wrong? Why haven't you been able to find a job?**

As you know with this economy, it's been a difficult market. I didn't realize what a challenge it would be. I've worked hard to get a few interviews, and I came close to getting an offer twice. The competition is stiffer than I thought it would be, and the opportunities are fewer. I have been an excellent employee in the past, and I will be again.

Q. This position with our company requires a college degree, and I noticed on your résumé you state only that you attended college, but it didn't say you graduated? Why did you quit?

I didn't get a chance to complete my degree because . . . (and it better be a good reason, like a death in the family . . . I was married with a kid and I had to go to work . . . I was putting myself through college and the money ran out, so I had to go to work.)

Do not say things like: "I was bored . . . college and I didn't get along . . . I didn't value the chance I had enough and I regret it." Even things like, "I just wasn't mature enough for college and didn't appreciate it," won't work. You must have a good, palatable reason for not completing your degree.

Then finish with this powerful phrase:

I do wish I'd finished, but every job I've ever had has required a degree on paper. I have performed well at all of them. In fact, when you analyze my background and check my refer-

ences, you will find that my not having a degree has never affected my performance.

Q. This position is one or two levels below the jobs you've had in the past. How do we know we won't hire you, and then in six or seven months someone calls you with a position like that and you leave? (This is one of the biggest fears that any hiring manager or hiring authority has. To hire somebody and then have them leave, for whatever reason, is a big risk.)

In every company where I've worked, I've started out at a position one or two levels below what I eventually attained. I have no intention of wasting anyone's time, money, or effort, especially mine or yours; I wouldn't be trying to get this position if I didn't think that it would be challenging, gratifying work and I wouldn't have a really good future with this organization.

Expand your answer by reassuring the hiring authority that you won't just jump at the next chance that comes your way.

In the past, I would get calls from time to time about interviewing at other organizations or other companies for higher-level positions. But I was very happy where I was. I enjoyed the work, I was challenged, and, frankly, the compensation followed my being happy, content, and challenged in the job.

Finally, zero in on what a great opportunity this is and say that you're sure they won't be disappointed.

If we can make this opportunity happen, I assure you I know exactly what I'm getting into and the idea of leaving, or being recruited away for another position, just isn't realistic for me. I like the job, the people, the company, and if we can work out the compensation, I am more than confident that I will make you an excellent employee for a long, long time.

Q. Why did you leave your last job so abruptly? . . . or . . . Why do you want to leave your current job? How do I know you won't do the same here? (This is one of the most difficult and treacherous questions you're going to be asked. The biggest mistake candidates make when it comes to this question is that they, first, don't mention how much they appreciate the job they had or presently have and then, secondly, they talk about self-centered reasons for either leaving or changing jobs.)

You know, I really loved that job for_____, and really appreciated all of the people whom I was working with. Unfortunately, the company had to downsize because of the economy and since I was one of the last hired, I was one of the first to go.

Another powerful phrase you can use in this situation is:

I really love my job and I love the people with whom I worked. But I've reached a point where the opportunity for me to grow both personally and professionally just isn't there. They are good people and have been good to me. I will certainly miss them, and I'm sure that they will miss me, but I am capable of greater responsibility and authority and the odds of me getting that where I am just aren't very great.

Never criticize, denigrate, bad-mouth, or in any way speak poorly of your present or past employer.

Q. Were you fired? And why were you fired? (I don't recommend that you answer this question with something like, "It's the best thing that ever happened to me . . . it was a blessing in disguise . . . the job wasn't working out, anyhow . . . the job just wasn't for me." These kinds of answers have a tendency to come across as flippant and arrogant.)

I really loved that job and the opportunity it afforded me. I learned a lot from those people, and the time I spent there was gratifying. Unfortunately, because of management changes and economic issues, we had to go through a layoff, and I happened to be one of the ones who was affected.

Now, if you were fired for any cause, even if you don't agree with it, you need to use this phrase:

I really loved that company. I performed well, but there came a time for us, the company and me, to make a change.

Then smile in a very friendly way, stop talking, and keep looking the interviewer in the eye. You can follow up with:

And before that, I was at _____ (company), where I performed very well.

If the cause of your dismissal was an external one, like going through a divorce, an illness, an illness in the family—something that is now behind you—you should use a phrase like:

Unfortunately I was going through a difficult divorce (or illness of my parents, spouse, and so forth), *and I was terribly distracted from my work. I missed a lot of work and wasn't very focused when I was there. We had to part ways, and I understand the reasons.*

Fortunately, I have emotionally recovered from the divorce and am ready to focus 100 percent on my new job. I have been an excellent employee before and will be one for you.

Answering this question, when you have no other choice but to admit you were fired, even for cause, takes more practice than probably any answer you will ever give in an interviewing situation. Practice! Practice! Practice!

Q. Where do you see yourself five years from now . . . or how does this job fit into your career goals? (If you answer anything along the lines of, "I have no idea," you're dead in the water. If you are too audacious and say something like, "I want be the president of this company," you'll appear foolish.)

I'm not sure of exactly what kind of position I will have in five years, but my goal is to be performing in a challenging position where my company feels like I'm contributing to its success, taking advantage of every attribute that I have. I feel that if I do the very best I can every day, push myself to the limit, grow personally and professionally, then tomorrow, as well as five years from now, will take care of itself.

Q. How much time did you take off last year? (Be truthful about this answer. After all, if a company checks your previous employment reference, one question they might ask will be about an excessive number of absences. So, if you were absent from work an inordinate amount of time in the past year, be sure to communicate that the circumstances were out of the ordinary and that being absent from work is not a habit for you.)

I'm a stickler for punctuality and being at work every day. In the last two years, there's been a lot of illness in our family, which caused me to be out more than normal. The situation has been rectified, and there's no reason that I wouldn't be at work every day.

Q. Have you ever had personal financial difficulties? (If you have had personal credit challenges caused by a bankruptcy, divorce, being out of work for so long, or any other less than positive circumstance, the best thing to do it is to admit that your credit has been "bruised" and enumerate the circumstances that caused the issue. If you think that a rough credit history may be an issue for a prospective employer, don't let him or her find out about it when they do a credit check.)

Unfortunately, in this last recession, I had some real problems with my credit. It has been bruised. But I have recovered and repaired the damage.

If you had to file bankruptcy, the phrase to use is:

You need to know that I have filed bankruptcy. However, I have repaired the damage and have had no challenges recently.

Q. If you inherited a lot of money, say $2 or $3 million, what would you do?

I worked all my life and no matter how much money I might have in the bank, I would foresee continuing to work.

No one really knows what they would do if they inherited a lot of money, so this really is a silly question. However, the hiring authority is afraid of hiring someone and then having that person soon quit, whatever the reason.

Q. This job pays $10,000 a year less than what you've been making. How do we know that you won't take the job and then keep looking to try to make up for that difference?

I see this as a career move. To me, money is not the primary reason for accepting or rejecting an offer. In fact, the last two jobs I accepted were at salaries that were less than other offers I had. I am motivated by my career, the challenge of the job, and the intrinsic value of doing well. If I do a good job, the money takes care of itself.

Q. If a personal commitment conflicts with a business emergency, what do you do? (This is a somewhat loaded question.)

Fortunately, I've never been caught in that bind. I've always been able to make sure that unexpected personal commitments have been taken care of by someone else. Because of my personal situation, I doubt that I would have to make that choice.

Q. If you could start your career over again, what would you do differently? (This is kind of a trick question. Whatever you do, don't go overboard about all the mistakes you've made and what you would have done differently.)

You know, I've been fortunate; I haven't made too many mistakes in my career, and I've sure learned a lot from the ones that I made. There aren't very many career choices or deci-sions that I would change.

Q. How long will you stay with us if you are hired or How do I know that you will stay with us for a reasonable period of time to be effective?

As you can see, I've been very stable in the positions I've had before, and I would expect that as long as the opportunity is fulfilling and the company is pleased with my work, I will stay just as long here. I have never really left my jobs so much as the jobs have left me for one reason or another.

Or you can use this powerful phrase:

My experience has been that as long as I'm challenged and the company I work for is pleased with my work, we both grow. As long as both of us are growing, there's no real need for either one of us to make a change.

Q. Have you ever been asked in any of your jobs to do something unethical? How did you handle it? (Tell the truth. In rare instances, candidates leave companies because they're asked to do unethical things. If you did leave because you were asked to do something unethical, don't make a big, long emotional harangue about how somebody asked you to "cheat" and you wouldn't do it. Simply use the following phrase.)

A few years ago, I was asked to account for an expense that really wasn't for a client. It made me uncomfortable enough to where I left the company within a few months. I considered it crossing the line, and the folks I worked directly for didn't see it that way.

You don't want to come across as "holier than thou" and show contempt for people who might ask you to do something out of line. Likewise, you need to make it clear that you didn't agree with what you were asked to do, so you refused to do it.

Q. You are awfully young for this position, aren't you? I'm afraid that, in building your career, you would only stay with us for a short period of time.

I know that I'm a bit young to have accomplished what I have, but I find that maturity is more an issue of experience and being able to perform than it is one of age. As long as I am contributing to the business endeavor of the organization and personally growing, there is no reason for me to leave.

Q. You are awfully young for this position, aren't you? (See the previous question. Without the statement that follows above, it may relate more to your fitting in than to your age. So, it might be a good idea to clarify the question in your response.)

I have found that maturity is more an issue of contributing to an organization than one of age. I have been fortunate enough to be in situations where I was able to contribute and grow. Are you asking this because there are few people in the organization my age?

Once you get the answer to your question, you can assure the interviewing or hiring authority that you have been in this situation before.

I have always been in departments where I have been younger than most anybody the group. In checking my refer-

ences you'll find that this has never been an issue—for them or for me.

Q. You will be older than anyone else here . . . how does that make you feel?

I have worked in organizations where I was older than the majority of the employees and it wasn't a problem. In fact, I've provided a great balance of experience that others didn't have. It was great.

Q. You will be younger than anyone else here . . . how does that make you feel?

I've worked in organizations where I was the youngest by far. In fact, I provided a great balance for the team.

Q. You live an awfully long way from here. It will take you at least forty-five minutes to get to work one way. With the price of gas, as well as your time, after a while, you might lose enthusiasm for the job!

I have had to commute before, and I am not bothered by it. In fact, it gives me a great opportunity to listen to motivational tapes and CDs. I use the time to learn and get better. If you check my references, you will find that I was rarely late for work.

Q. Were you ever denied a pay raise, got a poor performance review, or were passed up for a promotion? What did you do?

I've never had a poor performance review (be sure this is true) *and the one or two times in my career that I might have been passed over for promotion, it worked out best for the organization and therefore it worked out well for me. My experiences then have shown me that if I perform well pay raises, promotions, etc., always take care of themselves.*

Q. Do you object to psychological testing? (This is only going to be asked by an organization that does this kind of testing. If you object, you are probably going to be eliminated as a candidate.)

Not at all. I've taken them before.

Q. What do you think about _____ **(any controversial issue, for example, politics, religion, or anything in the news that might be controversial)?** (If it is something that is controversial, no matter what your opinion is, don't give it.)

You know I am trying to learn more about _____; I'd be interested to know what your opinion is.

Q. When do you plan on retiring? (This is especially difficult if you are over fifty-five or sixty years old.)

My goodness, I love working so much, I don't know that I would ever retire.

Q. You have been out of work for more than a year and have said that you could afford to do that. How do we know that if we hire you, you won't quit after three or four months since you obviously can afford not to work?

I was fortunate enough to be able to live frugally during that period of time. But it certainly wasn't an extravagant life-

style. I need to work not only emotionally and mentally, but also economically. I can't afford to stay out of the workplace any longer.

Q. Have you ever been involved in a lawsuit? Business or personal? (You have to answer this question very carefully. Lawsuits are usually public records even if they are settled. So, if you have been involved in a lawsuit, state that you have and give a very brief one- or two-sentence explanation about it. Then be quiet.)

In the businesses that I worked for, I have been involved in a few lawsuits.

Q. What will your boss say when you resign? Will he or she be upset? (This is a bit of a loaded question. It might be asked so that the interviewer can find out if you have confided in your present boss, or the interviewer just might throw the question out there to see how you react.)

I'm sure my boss will be somewhat disappointed, but he or she has always been the kind that wants what's best for everyone in the organization. If finding a new job is best for my family, and me, while my boss might be unhappy about the situation for the company, he (or she) will be pleased for me.

Q. This job and this company are real big risks. We don't know how long we're going to be able to make it. What do you think? (This is a question that comes up from time to time. Sometimes it is a question to test you to see if you are a risk taker.)

I am by nature a risk taker. I don't have a problem with a risky company or a risky opportunity as long as the rewards are there.

Q. Can we contact your references, including present and former employers? (The only problem with this question is that you might not want anyone checking your present employer as a reference until after you have left your job.)

I have no problem with you checking my previous employment references when we get to the proper offer stage. But I certainly would not want anyone checking my present employer as I have not left, and they have no idea that I'm looking for a job.

Q. Knowing what you know about the job you are interviewing for, what are the things that you're going to dislike the most?

Well, from what I know about, there might be some things that I may not like as well as others, but I haven't found anything that I would dislike.

Q. What is the least relevant job that you had? (Be pensive and think about this for a few moments.)

At just about every job I've ever had, I learned something. There were jobs during college and right out of college that weren't as relevant to my career growth as they could have been, but I sure learned a lot by working at them. I've always felt that, no matter how menial the task, I need to do my best.

Q. Sometimes people stretch the truth or don't tell the truth in order to protect themselves or their organization. Have you ever found it necessary to do this? (This is a really tough question. It ranks up there with the question "Do you ever lie?")

Part of being successful in business is being able to present things just as they are, for better or for worse. I've never been comfortable with covering up or stretching the truth. My memory isn't that good and in situations where I've seen people do this, it inevitably comes back to haunt them. My experience is that one lie leads to another and then leads to another, and they're never really to anyone's best interest.

Q. What is your energy level like? Describe one of your typical days. (You must always communicate that you have a high energy level. You do that by sitting up and leaning forward with relaxed intensity.)

I've always been told that I have a high degree of energy. I'm motivated to do a good job, and I've been blessed with the ability to work quickly and be able to maintain that level of energy nine to ten hours a day.

Describe your day by making sure you are up and at your job very early, undertaking a lot of activity, and going home later than most people. You have to communicate doing a lot of work and doing it quickly.

Q. Have you done the best work you are capable of doing? (This is a trick question. If you say that you have done the very best work you're capable of doing, it may come across as egotistical. If you say that you haven't done the best work you were capable of doing, you may come across as an underachiever.)

Based on the experience that I have had, I was doing the best work that I was capable of doing. The more experience that I have, the better my work gets.

Q. Can you work under pressure? Tell me about the most pressured situation you were in. (You should be able to relate a good story in answer to this question.)

A few years ago our company was struggling. We had a bank note coming due, and the president of our company sent me to a customer that would save the company if they bought from us. If they didn't, we would have been in terrible shape with the bank and likely lost the company. I was successful in getting a contract from the client. It saved the company.

Q. Describe the most difficult problem you had to deal with. (Watch out for this kind of question. It is better to describe a difficult business problem than a personal one. Again, a story is best.)

Over a period of four months I restructured our company's debt with four different vendors we owed money to because things were very tight. We made a deal with each one of them, and we are now each one's best customer.

Q. How do you manage to interview while still employed? (This is a question that's going to put you on the spot a bit regarding your integrity or character.)

I have accrued quite a bit of vacation, and I've been taking it to interview.

Don't be flippant or casual about the answer.

Q. When would you expect a promotion?

I have found in the past that promotions have come after I have performed successfully. In the past, I really haven't worried about promotions, because I know that if I do my job and I do it better than others, the opportunity to go beyond my position will present itself.

Q. What kinds of decisions are most difficult for you? (An answer that communicates compassion and empathy for other people is usually a good answer for this kind of question.)

It is difficult when I have to fire someone or lay them off, and I know it affects not only them but also other people. I have done it, and know that I'm going to have to continue to do it, but it still isn't easy.

Q. Your résumé shows that you been with one company a long time without any appreciable increase in rank or salary. Tell me about this.

I really love my job and the company that I work for. We aren't the kind of company that has a lot of turnover, so opportunities to get promoted have been very rare. My company has given salary increases when they can, but they have been strapped for the last few years.

One of the reasons that I am looking to leave is to experience personal and, therefore, economic growth. Frankly, that's why I'm interviewing with you and your firm.

Q. What area of your skills and professional development do you want to improve at this time? (Most people never think of this question until they get asked it in an interview. And that's the worst time to start thinking about the answer. Most professionals need to be working on their game all of the time. If you are a professional in, say, the technology area, you need to communicate that you are taking courses or improving your skills in some aspect of technology. If you are not in a profession where this kind of thing is that clear-cut, you need to communicate that you are constantly taking personal development and personal growth types of training.)

On a personal level, I am constantly reading and listening to motivational and inspirational CDs and books. On a professional level, I'm involved in two associations and try to take at least two daylong professional symposiums a year.

Q. Why should I hire you as an outsider when I could fill the job with someone inside the company? (This is a great question, and I am surprised that it doesn't get asked more often.)

My experience has been that if companies can find equal candidates internally as well as externally, they should look at hiring internally. But I have also found that hiring externally brings new blood, new ideas, and renewed energy to the organization, and it usually works out very well.

Q. How long have you been looking for another position?
(Hiring or interviewing authorities will be concerned if you have been on the job market too long. They will wonder, "What is wrong with this person." Be sure to give a logical and reasonable explanation of why you might still be looking. If you have been looking for a job for what might appear to be an inordinate amount of time, like six months or so, you have to answer this question with the statement that you are looking for the right opportunity.)

I've been actively looking for a position for the past few months, and although I've had a number of opportunities to accept a job, I haven't found the right match.

Q. What do you think of your current or last boss and previous bosses? (This is a great chance for you to shoot yourself in the 'foot. The metaphors and analogies that you give here are extremely important. No matter what—even if you were fired by the biggest jerk in the world—you absolutely have to present your current or last boss in positive terms.)

I've been very fortunate. I respected every boss that I've ever had and have learned an immense amount from each one of them. In one or two instances, I didn't particularly like my boss, but I appreciated everything I learned from them. For the most part, though, I've had really great bosses.

Q. What would you do when you have a great deal of work to accomplish in a short time span? How have you reacted to that situation? (Be ready to answer this question with an appropriate story.)

I am constantly setting goals and planning. So, I set priorities for myself and for others. If I have a great deal of work to accomplish in a short time span, I have to analyze my priorities and pick the ones that are most important.

Years ago, I reacted too emotionally and tried to get all of it done. I have found that, in cases like this, unless someone can put twenty-six hours in a day, I have to decide what the priorities are and act on them.

Q. Tell me about a time when your team fell apart. Why did it happen? What did you do? (Again, to reinforce your ability to deal with stress and strain you need a story or two.)

Our accounting apartment was under a deadline to get a due diligence report to the CEO. There were five of us in the department. Two people quit, and one had to take leave for a family emergency. It didn't look like we were going to get the report done on time.

Years ago, I would have panicked. But in this case, I called the two people that had quit and hired them as independent contractors for two weekends. I then hired a contract accountant to organize the report. I asked the CEO for a two-day grace period, which she granted. We made the new deadline and produced a great report.

Q. How did you feel about your workload at that company? (Never, ever complain about your workload. Explain that you appreciated the amount of work you were assigned, and that all of the best managers seemed to have a lot on their plate.)

I don't think I've ever felt overloaded—maybe overwhelmed at moments, but never overloaded. The way I've avoided this is to always make a plan, and then work it in a calm, deliberate manner. Now, it may take long evenings and some weekends and a lot of focus time, but planning is the key.

Q. After I get to know you, what will annoy me about you? (Don't take this bait.)

Well, although I try to work at it, I'm not a very good golfer (or tennis player or bowler or poker player or . . .).

Then smile. Don't get into anything more personal than this. It simply can't help you.

Q. I see you are working on your MBA (or graduate) degree. What are you going to do when you get it? (Some companies really like people getting graduate degrees and some don't care. It is helpful if you know how many of the managers or people in the organization have MBA or graduate degrees.)

I decided to pursue an MBA (or graduate degree) *as much for personal growth as anything else. In my experience, I have seen that having an MBA* (or graduate degree) *doesn't necessarily make you a better professional. But, I am a constant learner and if it helps along the way, it will be of value.*

Q. Wow! Your grades are really low! What happened? (Take this question very seriously.)

It did take me a couple of years to really get focused on college (or graduate school). *I was very active in college in organizations and had leadership positions. I also had to work to earn money for college and its expenses. If I had to do it again, I would probably work a little harder.*

If your college or graduate school was more than a couple of years ago, mention that your job performance has been excellent throughout your working years.

Q. We found that you have had a number of DWIs. Can you explain? (It is best that you inform the hiring authority about your having DWIs before they are discovered with a background check.)

Unfortunately, there was a time when I wasn't as disciplined as I am now. That was a while ago, and I assure you nothing like that will happen again in the future.

If the DWI has been recent, be able to show that you are enrolled in or have completed a rehabilitation program and are receiving ongoing therapy or membership and participation in AA.

Q. You are coming back into the workforce after giving birth to a child. How do I know you won't work for a while and then decide to stay with the baby?

My family and I always expected that I would go back to work. We have great childcare (preferably, a family member). *I am punctual and I need to work. My career is very important to me, and that's why I'm interviewing with your organization.*

Q. You relocated here because of the job market. How do we know that when the market becomes better, you won't return to your old town?

My family and I made a conscious effort to move here and put down roots. Where I moved from has limited potential and my family there totally understands us moving here. We have family in the area as well as good friends. Back home is a nice place to visit, but we don't want to live there.

Q. You are changing careers. How do we know that if we hire you, you may not like your new career and go back to what you were doing before?

Changing careers is a deliberate, conscious business decision. The career I had before has a very limited future. I know that I'll have to take two or three steps backward in order to move forward. But I also know that I am going to be just as successful in this new career as I was in my last one. It will take a few years for me to get to the level I was before, but I'm absolutely confident I will. I've researched this new career as well as your company, and I know it's the right thing for me.

HOW THIS AFFECTS YOU

When hiring authorities hire an employee who doesn't work out, they look bad. No matter how many people are involved in the hiring decision, the immediate hiring authority is held responsible for a poor decision. The fear of making a poor hiring decision is a much greater motivator than the hope of a good hiring decision.

If a hiring authority has an equal number of good reasons to hire a candidate and good reasons to not hire a candidate, the candidate will never get hired. Because of the risk, a hiring authority is going to err on the side of safety and may pass up an excellent candidate for a lesser person who has fewer risks.

The vast majority of candidates don't recognize the risk they pose to the hiring authority. You need to be sure that you think critically about what risks you may pose to a potential employer. Ask your spouse or a close friend about your risk factors. Get their honest opinion. This will help you successfully prepare for interview questions about your weaknesses, difficult situations, and problems in your background.

7

Powerful Phrases for Successful Follow-Up Interviews

So you've made it past the first interview and now you've been called back for a second one. You should be congratulated for making it past the initial interview since 90 to 95 percent of the candidates don't make it that far. But the process is not over by a long shot. Now you have to really step up your game because the competition is tougher, and the hiring authorities want to determine who the best candidate is from among the very good ones.

Job seekers, more often than not, make mistakes in the interviewing process beyond the initial interview. Here are the most critical ones:

→ *They think that that because they have been invited back, they're going to get hired.* This is just another step in the process. Managing the steps at this stage is different from handling the initial interview.

→ *They treat subsequent interviews in the same way that they treated an initial interview.* Although the basic presentation is the same, follow-up interviews need to be customized and refined to do them correctly.

→ *They don't get a clear idea of how many other candidates are being moved to the next step and what their backgrounds are.* The competition is now keener. You have to get a really good idea about how many other candidates you are competing against, what their backgrounds are, and how you stack up against them.

→ *They don't solicit the help of the initial interviewer in "promoting" them to the next step.* Talk with the initial interviewing authority to find out everything you can about the subsequent interviews. How many interviews will there be? Who will the interviews be with?

→ *They aren't clear about how the subsequent interviews might differ from the initial interviews.* Ask the initial interviewing authority questions like: "What will be the main focus of the follow-up interviews?" "Beyond what I communicated to you in the initial interview, what more will they want?" "What are the strengths I should highlight or weaknesses I should bolster in the subsequent interviews?" Get the idea? You can't assume that follow-up interviews will be like the initial interviews.

→ *They don't research the company, the position, and the people doing the subsequent interviewing in even more depth than for the initial interview.* Since you now have a better idea of what the company might want in hiring someone, you should do more in-depth research about the job, those who will be interviewing you, and anything else that might be pertinent.

→ *They don't expend some kind of "going the extra mile" effort in subsequent interviews.* Any kind of activity or effort that will set you apart from the other candidates in subsequent interviews is great. Be prepared to demonstrate your ability to do the job. I encourage candidates to develop thirty-, sixty-, and ninety-day plans as to what they would do in the first ninety days of employment and pass them out in follow-up interviews.

→ *They relax and forget that it's in subsequent, follow-up interviews where most candidates get eliminated.* You must interview better and work harder in follow-up interviews than you did in the initial interviews. This is not the time to take your foot off the gas and start coasting.

→ *They neglect to get the support of the subsequent interviewing authorities. This means asking every interviewing or hiring authority in follow-up interviews if they are going to endorse your being hired.* You must ask, "What do I need to do to get the job?" and "Will you support my candidacy over the other candidates?" It is crucial that you get "buy-in" from the people with whom you interview. You want them to support you as a candidate.

→ *They don't realize how crucial subsequent interviews are.* You have to interview better than you did on the initial interviews. I often refer to follow-up interviews as the playoffs. Once you've gotten through the initial interview, the competition really heats up. Now you definitely have to bring your A game.

Most candidates simply assume that subsequent interviews beyond the initial interview are going to be just like the initial one. I've even had candidates over the years call me after an initial interview and actually say, "Tony, I got the job. They're having me back for a second and third interview." They couldn't miscalculate things any greater.

Candidates often have no idea that the subsequent interviewing process is most likely much more difficult and treacherous than the initial interview. They aren't ready for the kind of intensity and complication that goes on in the follow-up process. This part of the process is much less predictable and patterned than any other stage in the interviewing process.

WHAT TO EXPECT

You absolutely must be aware that the follow-up interviewing process is going to be very different from what you experienced in the initial interviewing process. You're going to basically sell yourself in the same way; but there are going to be a greater number of variables in this process than there were in the initial interview. Just be ready and know that it is a brand-new day and a brand-new process; *just because you made it past the initial interview, you can take nothing for granted.* Be prepared for playoff intensity, because now it's all on the line just like in the playoffs.

Remember, I stated earlier that the interviewing process is a staged and contrived event. Well, the reason that most organizations involve so many people in the hiring decision is to *spread the risk.* Yes, you read it right. Corporate America will tell you that the reason so many people interview a candidate for a job is that the more people involved in the decision, the better the decision. Employers say they want to make sure of the candidate's qualifications: that he or she can do the job, that everybody likes the person, and so forth. But the truth is that no one individual wants to take on the responsibility of making a poor hiring decision and personally have to live with the possibly bad consequences. People in the hiring process are so afraid of making a mistake that if they do, they want other people to share the responsibility for the screw-up.

Now let's cover power phrases to be used when you get beyond the initial interview.

When the First Interviewer Is Not the Hiring Authority

If your initial interview is conducted by a third party or simply an interviewing authority, and you make it past this person to the second stage of interviewing, you are most likely one of the safest candidates to be interviewed. The interviewer who does not have hiring authority is usually going to screen out far more candidates than are allowed to go forward. This person is going to look for more reasons why a candidate *should not* be considered than reasons why the candidate *should* be considered. As I've stated before, these people don't want to look bad.

Once the interviewing authority has told you that you're going to be promoted to the next step in the process, you need to be sure that you get this person's support for future interviews within the company. Here is the power phrase to use:

Mr. or Ms._____, I really want this job and am convinced that I am the best candidate you could hire. I would like you to help me as much as you can through the interviewing process.

Even if you have to suggest meeting a second time before you go on the subsequent interviews, you want them to share as much information as possible so that you perform well in the rest of the interviewing process. Here are several power phrases you can use:

Based on my experience and the interview with you, do you have any concerns about, first, my ability to do the job, and secondly, my ability to perform well with the other people that I will meet?

Please give me as much information as possible about the next person I would be interviewing with. Who are they? What is their role in the position? How many people will I be interviewing with? Please describe the whole process.

How many other candidates will you be speaking with at the next level of interviews? In your opinion, how do I stack up with the other candidates? What are my strengths? What are my weaknesses?

In your opinion how do I rank with the other candidates. Am I first, second, or third in your opinion?

What has set me apart from the candidates that you did not schedule to move forward?

What in your opinion do I need to do to get the job?

As I go through the interviewing process, I'd like to ask you if you could coach me through it. You obviously have a lot of knowledge of the company and the people in it, and I'd like you to help me. Is there a time when we might meet either in person or on the phone?

When the First Interviewer *Is* the Hiring Authority

Studies have shown that successful hires are just as likely if *only* the hiring authority is involved, as opposed to several people. In fact, one study I read documented that in certain industries and professions, it's actually better to have only one person, the hiring authority who is responsible for the position, involved in the interviewing process. But nobody is ever going to be able to convince corporate America that they are just as well-off when one person does the interviewing and hiring as they are when several people are involved in the process.

This is a much easier situation to deal with than when the

first interviewer is not a hiring authority. When the hiring authority does the interviewing, he or she takes on long-term, personal responsibility for the decision. Most of the time, this person is going to be responsible for not only hiring you, but also contributing to your success or lack of it in the job. This person's reputation is really on the line.

When hiring authorities decide to move candidates up in the interviewing process, they are getting other opinions in order to protect themselves. Since hiring is a personal thing and these people have a personal, vested interest in whoever is successful in getting the job, they are likely to help you as much as they can. So, here are the power phrases you should use:

I'm excited about the opportunity to move along in the interviewing process. Thank you! I really want this job and want to do everything I can to get it. So, could you please explain to me the rest of the hiring process? How many people will be involved? When would you like to make a decision?

Do you have any concerns about my ability to do the job? In your opinion, what are my strengths? What are my weaknesses?

How many other candidates are going beyond the interview that I had with you? How do I stack up with those other candidates? If you were to compare me with the other candidates, how would I rank?

Who are the other people that I will be meeting with? I'd like to do research on them. What is their role in the decision-making process? Individually, what might they like or not like about my background? Can you describe their personalities? What is their relationship with you and the job that I am applying for?

Provided I do well in the next series of interviews, do

*you have any concerns about my ability to do the job? Will
you hire me?*

*I really want this job, and I would like to go to work for
not only the company, but with you personally. Can you
help coach me for the people I will speak with during the
rest of the interviewing process?*

*Can you tell me about the people I will be meeting
with? Do they have any pet peeves . . . prominent things
that they like or don't like . . . things I need to be concerned about?*

*Based on our interview, are there any things that I
should clarify about my experience or background with
the next interviewing authority? Do you think this person
will have any concerns about my ability or my experience?*

Multiple Interviews

Mark my word, and you better remember this: The more people
who are involved in the interviewing process, the more difficult
it is going to be to get hired.

I am constantly amazed at the number of interviewing authorities above the hiring authority who have a completely different idea about what kind of candidate should be hired than
the initial hiring authority does. You would think that once an
organization decided it needed a particular type of individual,
all the people involved in the hiring decision would be reading
from the same page, and have some consistent idea among them
about what kind of person they ought to hire. Unfortunately,
most of the time this just isn't the case.

In the past few years, I'd say the average number of interviews
that you'll go through to get hired is four. But, over the years I
have seen as many as ten different interviewing authorities involved in one hiring decision. However, for most professional po-

sitions if your initial interview is with a screener, you will interview with four different authorities. It is a good idea if you are called back for a second interview to find out how many interviews there will be in the process by using the power phrases mentioned previously.

Time Is Your Enemy

The longer the interviewing process takes, and the more people who are involved in it, the less likely it is that you, or anyone else for that matter, will get hired. There is no normal time period that is standard for the interviewing process. I have experienced interviewing/hiring processes that took fifteen minutes, and I have experienced ones that took eighteen months; and some that got started but then ended with no one being hired.

One of the issues you're going to have to deal with in the interviewing process is the *paradox of urgency*. The paradox of urgency states that every interviewing and hiring authority absolutely, unequivocally, urgently has to fill his or her position . . . someday. Most interviewing or hiring authorities whom you interview with will act as though filling the position you are interviewing for is the most important thing they can be doing; that it is their number-one priority; and that they are going to set everything aside until they're successful at finding the perfect candidate. But it just isn't so.

SUCCESS PLANS FOR FOLLOW-UP INTERVIEWS

The strategy for follow-up interviews is not far off from the strategy that you used in the initial interview. To a certain extent, you're going to do exactly what you did in the initial interview with a couple of added steps to give you the advantage. Again, the process is simple, but most people don't think to do it.

When you get to interviews beyond the initial interview, you will basically give the same kind of presentation about yourself that you gave to the person that did the initial interview. You will want to take into account everything you learned about the next people that you are interviewing with: their likes, dislikes, and concerns. In a way, you will want to customize your presentation based on what you learned about them from the previous interviewer. It is not easy, but it is simple enough.

Whether you have just one interview beyond the initial interview or nine interviews, you need to gain as much information as you possibly can about the people that you are interviewing with. The best way to do that is to pick the brain of each individual interviewer before you go to the next level. Find out as much information about subsequent interviewers as you possibly can. Ask about their professional life, their personal life, their family, their hobbies, their personal likes or dislikes—whatever the initial interviewer is willing to share. You never know what even minor detail you might have in common with the next interviewing authority that will set you apart from the other candidates.

Remember. You're going to give the same basic presentation about yourself to everyone you interview with. You're going to treat them just exactly the same way as you did the initial interview authority. As you wind down the interview, you use these power phrases:

Thank you for meeting with me. I really appreciate the opportunity. Please tell me how I stack up with the other candidates you have interviewed.

Do you have any concerns about my ability to do the job you are hiring for?

Have I made my experience and ability clear to you?
How do I stack up with the other candidates that you
have interviewed?
What do I need to do to get the job?

In sales terminology, you are "closing" the sale. You are doing everything you can to get the support of the person that you are interviewing with. No matter how many second, third, fourth, and fifth interviewing authorities beyond the initial interview you speak with, they are going to have a say in your being hired. Don't be duped by any of them saying to you, "Well, I'm really not important in the hiring decision. They asked me to interview you as a courtesy." Don't buy it! If the people you're speaking with couldn't say no and eliminate you as a candidate, they wouldn't be interviewing you.

Now, after you ask this last question, don't be surprised if the interviewing authority says something like, "Well, I'm really leaving the decision up to the direct hiring manager. So, I will get with him or her and give my input."

If you hear this kind of thing—and it's likely you will—you have to use this power phrase:

Mr. or Ms. _____, it is obvious that your opinion
means something, or I wouldn't be interviewing with you.
From what I understand you are highly respected in the
organization. Do I have your support? Are you going to
tell Mr. or Ms. _____ to hire me?"

This is a phenomenally powerful phrase. It is aggressive, direct, and to the point. The interviewing authority may very well try to beg off by saying something like, "Well, it really isn't my decision." If you hear something like this, you need to use this power phrase:

I understand your position, but it's important for me to know that I have your support and your vote. I'm sure the hiring authority will ask your opinion, and I need to know I have your support."

I can't emphasize enough how important it is for you to use this line of questioning. I also can't tell you, unfortunately, how many candidates over the years, to whom I have taught these power phrases, can't quite bring themselves to use them. Because they fear rejection, they don't use them and give me the namby-pamby excuse, "Well, it just didn't seem appropriate." Or something like, "It just didn't seem like the right time to say that." What this tells me is they didn't have the courage to ask the cold, hard question: "Are you going to hire me?"

The higher up the management chain you interview, the more this kind of respectful bluntness will be appreciated. Decision makers love it when candidates use these kinds of qualifying phrases. In fact, don't be surprised if the interviewing authority smiles and says something like, "You are the only candidate I've interviewed so far that has asked me these questions. I appreciate your courage."

Even if you don't get the answer of, "Yes, I will support you," you will definitely be remembered by the interviewing authority. This kind of courage is the kind of thing that decisive hiring managers really appreciate. And they don't hear it very often.

Don't forget to write thank-you e-mails to these interviewing authorities in the same way you did with the initial interviewing authorities. Reiterate why you were a great candidate and a few reasons as to why they want to hire you. Be specific; *don't* write something vague like this: "I am a qualified candidate. This is an excellent opportunity for both your firm as well as myself. I would do a great job. I would appreciate your vote and your support."

Many people get to a second, third, or fourth interview and think that since they have gotten this far, they have a lock on the job offer. They relax in their intensity, alter their presentation, and basically quit selling, thinking it's a done deal. This is a terrible mistake!

At each succeeding interview, you should present yourself in exactly the same manner as you did with the initial interview. If your system is working, don't mess with it. You should only alter your technique based on what the immediate interviewer might tell you about the next interviewer.

If the initial and subsequent interviewing authorities make suggestions about your presentation, make sure you alter your presentation to incorporate their ideas. Keep in mind that if interviewing authorities promote you to the next stage of the interviewing process, they have at least stated that you might be a viable candidate. If you ask the right questions as I have suggested, you'll not only get their support, but you will get their input and suggestions on how you might be able to interview successfully up the ladder.

Once you have completed each subsequent interview, follow up with e-mails, letters, and phone calls, if appropriate. I would not recommend calling an interviewing authority whose job is to simply "gut check" or provide another opinion in the interviewing process unless you bonded with him really well. You *do* want to phone the actual hiring authority and ask him or her about the decision. The more aggressive and assertive you are about selling yourself and closing on being the candidate who should be hired, the better off you are. You can be pushy, assertive, and confident without being obnoxious. Follow your gut, but don't be afraid you will lose the opportunity because you are too aggressive.

8
Powerful Phrases for Specific Professions and Positions

In this chapter I will discuss questions that would be asked for specific positions or professions in interviewing situations. (The job titles and/or descriptions are presented in alphabetical order to make them easier to find.) Naturally, you will have at your command the ability to discuss the specialized aspects of your field. The powerful phrases here are designed to apply to a broad range of questions in a particular discipline or role within a company.

ACCOUNTANT

Q. What makes you a good accountant?

My work is accurate, on time, and I interface well with other departments by appreciating what they do and their particular challenges and promoting the idea of "I'm here to help. What can I do to make your life easier?"

ADMINISTRATIVE PERSONNEL

Q. What do you consider your administrative strengths?

Punctuality . . . also I'm always at work. I hardly ever miss a day . . . I work fast and accurately and can take on responsibility beyond the scope of my job.

ADVERTISING

Q. Describe the most successful advertising campaign you designed (or worked on) and the one that was the least successful . . . and why wasn't it successful?

The most significant one—and it's easy to remember big wins—is a $1 million project we did eighteen months ago that directly led to one of the company's most successful product launches.

The biggest flop was something I was involved in five years ago. It flopped because of two major assumptions we made that turned out to be very wrong. I sure learned from that . . . lessons that are indelibly imprinted in my mind. I never take nor allow my team to take anything for granted— especially assumptions.

ARCHITECT

Q. Have you recently worked on a building of this scope?

Yes. I am a registered architect, NCARB-certified and LEED AP with fifteen years' experience at two firms involved in aviation (or healthcare, education, and so forth) projects with the title of senior project manager. I just finished a building very similar to the one you want to construct looking at this set of drawings. We brought it in six weeks early and under budget by $1.2 million.

ARCHITECTUAL DRAFTER

Q. We have interviewed a number of good drafters, what makes you different?

I am an AutoCAD guru with twelve years' experience. I'm working now with the new 3D version of Autodesk 3D 2013 and Revit.

ATTORNEY

Q. What distinguishes you from other trial attorneys you've seen in the courtroom?

I'm a tough, tenacious, and really smart litigator with a proven track record of receiving outstanding verdicts on behalf of my clients.

While I am recognized as being able to think quickly on my feet in high-pressure trial environments, I feel that my greatest strengths lie in my ability to create winning trial strategies, and to then meticulously plan, prepare, and execute them.

AUDITOR

Q. What do you think the most important skills are for an auditor?

To be well organized, and I have previous work papers to prove that I am . . . concise written skills, the ability to meet deadlines, attention to detail, good business acumen, and, most important, the ability to communicate with other businesspeople in terms they understand.

BANK PRESIDENT

Q. What do you feel makes a good president?"

First and foremost would be integrity and character. Obviously, qualifications and experience would be second. I think just as important is work ethic. In today's society, especially with the younger generation, the work ethic is a little lacking. These are the three qualities I feel make a good president. You have to lead the team and lead by example.

BOOKKEEPER

Q. What, in your opinion, makes the difference between a good bookkeeper and an excellent one?

I don't see my position as a job. I see my job as a career. I take personal responsibility as well as pride in what I do, even in the most mundane aspects of the job. I have found that the excellent bookkeepers I've interacted with all perform the same way.

BUSINESS ANALYST

Q. What's the most difficult challenge ahead for today's business analyst? And how does your background prepare you for it?

Business analysts must evaluate and synthesize information provided by a large number of people who interact with the business, such as customers, staff, IT professionals, and executives. We also work to facilitate communication between organizational units.

Then describe what you feel is the hardest thing to deal with and how you have handled this challenge in your career as a business analyst.

The biggest challenge facing most business analysts today is the rapid expansion and contraction of business organizations. I've experienced two companies that downsized and one very big merger. My ability to get all the departments to communicate and understand what's going on got me a promotion and the best performance review in the department.

CHEMIST

Q. What are the three most important attributes of a chemist?

Curiosity, concentration on detail, and being able to work independently without a lot of supervision.

CHIEF FINANCIAL OFFICER (CFO)

Q. What are the three most important skills that a CFO needs to possess?

A successful CFO must be a good strategist and have a clear, articulate understanding of how finance fits the mission of the company. A CFO must be a good translator/interpreter and communicate to everybody in the company a financial strategy in terms they all understand, and the CFO must be a leader . . . articulate and charismatic enough for people to follow.

CHIEF INFORMATION OFFICER (CIO)

Q. What is the biggest failing of most CIOs?

The biggest failing that most CIOs have is the inability to not only communicate and build relationships with the rest of the C-suite, but have an open door and dialogue with the other departments. So often, the IT department seems to be out on an island by itself.

COLLECTIONS MANAGER

Q. What is the biggest mistake you've learned from in managing the collections department?

The biggest mistake I've seen collections departments make is to not have very specific, clear policies that everybody knows and practices. I found that when we insist on a specific system and follow it, collections go up and even those that owe money appreciate our system.

CONSTRUCTION MANAGEMENT

Q. What is your typical management process for a construction job?

I receive approved building plans, reach out to subconsultants for bids, value engineer bids, establish contract, begin trades in standard construction fashion, describe points of inspection with the subs, review and approve pay apps, set up product warranties, turn over the project to the operations for final inspection, correct any items discovered by the operations team, and move on to the next project.

CONTROLLER

Q. What makes a good controller?

A good controller is a person who understands the financial aspects of the company to the last detail and can clearly explain them to every department in the company, so those departments see his or her role as supporting and facilitating their mission.

CORPORATE RECRUITER

Q. What would be your most immediate contribution to the company, if you were hired?

I produce quality candidates quickly based on the needs of the hiring authorities. I use a number of recruiting tools, Boolean searches, personal contacts, LinkedIn, and, fortunately, I have a phenomenal database of contacts. After that, I work really, really hard and really fast.

CREATIVE ARTS

Q. How do you sustain creativity?

Earlier in my career, I learned good habits from as many creative people as I could . . . reading, listening, studying, and absorbing every aspect of what creative people do. Now, I find that little things, like the mood I'm in, the people who are around me, and intrinsic motivation to be creative, keep me in a creative mood.

CREDIT MANAGER

Q. What is the greatest mistake you've made as a credit manager?

In my very first job as a credit manager, I had been promoted into the position when my boss retired . . . the two owners were brothers, and one of them operated with very little regard for credit policies. I guess I felt intimidated by him. One *of his better customers got far behind in paying us. I wasn't insistent enough in letting the brothers know how far behind the customer had gotten . . . almost $100,000.*

Always end by explaining what you learned from the mistake:

We ended up getting paid, but if I would have intervened sooner with strong policies, we wouldn't have run into the problem. I learned then to make very clear policies and get everyone's buy-in.

CUSTOMER SERVICE

Q. Give us an example of your success in customer service.

In my last two positions, I was always given the most difficult customers . . . the ones that were threatening lawsuits. I have a tremendous amount of natural empathy, as well as great training in dealing with customer issues. I pride myself on being technically competent and communicate a tremendous degree of understanding. I'm also very efficient and seem to be able to deal with more customer issues than most. I truly love my job.

EDITOR

Q. What are the attributes of a great editor?

Clarity, intellectual courage, a healthy ego but not an inflated one, a mastery of the English language, a realization that my job is to help writers look good, and, as important as anything, having the people skills to not bruise the authors' egos while helping their writing become more clear.

ENGINEER

Q. How would you rate yourself compared to other engineers?

I would compare myself very highly. I have a unique ability to see things from an engineering point of view, but also to be able to communicate well with nontechnical and business professionals.

ENTRY LEVEL POSITION

Q. How do we know that you'll be a hard worker and that you will be successful here?

I've been successful at everything I've ever done since I was fourteen. I was very successful in high school. Then I was very successful in college. I worked hard in high school and college, and got involved in a lot of social and leadership roles. I'm confident that I will be successful here.

ENVIRONMENTAL ENGINEER

Q. What were the biggest challenges in your last position as an environmental engineer?

The reason I am a good environmental engineer is that I inte-grate science and engineering to improve the natural environment and, more important, I am able to communicate that with the nontechnical people in the companies I have been with.

Once you've explained why you're good at what you do, discuss the challenges and how you've handled them.

Environmental engineering is often looked at as a compliance department, making people do what they don't want to do to comply with laws and so on. I am great at getting nontechnical people to understand how the contribution of environmental engineering is actually good for their business.

FINANCIAL ANALYST

Q. What is the difference between a good financial analyst and an exceptional one?

A good financial analyst will be able to collect and analyze all of the data pertinent to the project. An exceptional financial analyst offers opinions and strategies based on the philosophical foundation of the organization they are working for.

GRAPHIC DESIGN

Q. What makes a great graphic designer?

A lot of what a great graphic designer produces is subject to artistic interpretation. The great graphic designers are great artists, have great skills with composition and tools and software, and they understand business and marketing; they can visualize a great outcome. And they have a great work ethic.

HOTEL MANAGEMENT

Q. If we were to hire you, what would be the first few things that you would do?

The very first thing I would do is to quietly, in a low-key way, meet with all of the staff. I want to find out what's going on with the property, and the people who are actually interacting with the guests will know that best.

After I get a thorough assessment through the people working there, I would analyze the P&L of the property.

Doing those two things will give me a good foundation and a good start. I want to make this kind of assessments before I recommend any changes.

HUMAN RESOURCES

Q. What do you believe is the role of the HR department in relation to the mission, vision, and strategies of the business?

The HR department needs to be integral in manpower planning; managing the hiring and termination process; handling wage, salary, and benefits assessments; and overseeing the administration of performance appraisals, record keeping and compliance, employee welfare and motivation, labor relations, and employment policies.

INDUSTRIAL ENGINEERING

Q. What makes you a good industrial engineer?

Not only do I have a good track record of making processes more effective, more efficient, and safer, I have been really good at getting my ideas integrated into the people side of the organizations I have worked for.

The people I've worked with don't see me as an industrial engineer so much as they see me as somebody who helps make their life better by integrating my suggestions and ideas into their everyday work life.

INFORMATION TECHNOLOGY

Q. What sets you apart from the other successful IT candidates we have interviewed?

I'm a student of my profession. I truly love what I do. When I'm not doing it, I'm thinking about it. I'm always taking extra courses and seminars to keep me up on what I love.

INSIDE SALES

Q. How would you describe a successful inside salesperson?

First of all, someone with very high energy to make lots of calls. Secondly, someone bright enough to know who to call and what to say with very little direction. Thirdly, someone motivated enough to push themselves without being micromanaged.

INSIDE SALES MANAGER

Q. What makes a successful inside sales manager?

Recruiting and hiring the best people available . . . training and compensating them well, but also making them feel good about what they're doing and making them feel special . . . hitting a reasonable quota . . . letting the folks that work for me know that I have their back and push them gently and firmly.

LEGAL ASSISTANT

Q. How do we know you will work well under pressure?

It seems that every firm or attorney that I've ever worked for saved everything to the last minute . . . the last minute before depositions, trials, even settlement negotiations. I learned that I have to accept that we are running on Mach speed all the time.

I stay calm, take a deep breath, and don't get emotionally distracted. I focus on the goal and write out plans to reach the goal. I seem to provide a calming tone to an intense environment.

LOGISTICS MANAGEMENT

Q. What is the major contribution of logistics management to our business?

The real opportunity in supply chain and logistics is to understand your trading partners and be conscious of the cost savings that the department can control. With efficiency, the logistics department becomes an integral part of maximizing the ROI.

MACHINIST

Q. What are the three most important traits of a good machinist?

The first is to be dependable . . . so many people in my line of work are undependable. Second, practice a lot and rely on your experience. Third, be a student of the work and teach others when possible.

MARKETING

Q. What is the most significant accomplishment you have had in the last three years?

In the last three years, I've managed two major marketing projects. I delivered both of them before the deadline and well under budget. Both projects led to significant revenue and profit.

MORTGAGE BANKER

Q. What are the most important things you've learned that make you a good mortgage banker?

The best mentor I ever had told me that the difference between a good mortgage banker and an excellent mortgage banker is that the excellent one asks for and works mostly off of referrals. He or she listens to the clients, guides them, and works for them. After that it's a numbers game . . . the more people you talk to, the better you do.

NETWORK ENGINEER

Q. We've had some problems with our networks. What can you do to make them more reliable?

I'm a self-motivated network engineer with proven abilities and expertise in architecting, implementing, and troubleshooting a wide variety of cost-effective complex network and security solutions that really work. I take ownership of my space so you don't have to worry about it.

NURSE

Q. What made you become a nurse?

I truly love people and what I can do to help them. I'm a natural caregiver. Even before I got into the profession, I loved every one of my courses and graduated with excellent

*grades. Since then, I've worked in a number of different de-
partments in a number of different settings, had very diverse
nursing jobs, and I've loved every one of them.*

OPERATIONS MANAGER

Q. Our firm is three times the size of any organization you have worked for; how do we know you can do our job?

*While it is true that I have worked in smaller firms than yours,
the basic principles are the same. In checking my references,
you will find that I am very careful in budget projections,
supply-chain management, people management, and efficiency.*

*In every place that I have ever worked, I've seen that
things have run smoothly and economically. The size of the
organization and projects are relative, but the principles of
success are the same.*

PARALEGAL

Q. Why did you choose to pursue a career in the legal field?

*I want to work in a fast-paced environment that offers me a
wide range of experience and knowledge. As a paralegal, I
enjoy supporting different attorneys and acting as a liaison
to the clients who are usually under extreme duress.*

PHYSICAL THERAPIST

Q. What are the biggest drawbacks to being a physical therapist or challenges that you have experienced?

I'm naturally a caregiver and really want to help people. It gets frustrating when I teach people what to do and they don't practice it. Being patient when that happens is probably my biggest challenge. I strive to build great rapport with people, and most of my clients really appreciate what I do for them. Sometimes I wish I could help more.

PLANT AND PRODUCTION OPERATIONS

Q. What's been the most difficult challenge for you to handle?

We had some big changes in our manufacturing process over the last two years. Rather than implement them quickly and cause widespread confusion, I instituted a program to make the changes gradually and slowly. By doing it this way, we didn't interrupt our process of getting the products out on time, but we also kept people from being overwhelmed and therefore frustrated with change.

PUBLIC RELATIONS

Q. Give me an example where you turned a bad PR event into something worthwhile.

A few years ago, one of our plants had a terrible chemical leak. The press gave a lot of attention to it . . . even the EPA got involved. Fortunately, I had established a good working relationship with all of the media. We turned it into a positive. We immediately admitted our mistake, cleaned it up, and started a foundation for the environment in our part of the state.

QUALITY ASSURANCE

Q. What's been the biggest challenge of your career in quality assurance and how did you deal with it?

When I took over the department in my last company, we were known as the "no" department because the department had stood in everyone's way. I established standards of quality, reliability, safety, and effectiveness and communicated them to not just our department, but to all of the departments, even marketing. Now, our department is seen as an integral part of the team. We are even asked to participate in policy making in other departments.

QUALITY CONTROL

Q. You don't have as much experience as we would like. Why should we hire you?

The excellence I've shown throughout my career so far is what's most important. I changed quality programs at two organizations. The quality procedures I developed became a national standard for the firm.

RETAIL MANAGEMENT

Q. What do you think the biggest challenge for retailers is?

With the challenge of the Internet, retailers have to develop value-added relationships with customers. Customers have to have a great experience coming to our stores.

SALES

Q. What makes you a good salesperson?

I am intrinsically motivated. I know how to work the numbers. In the last four years, I have never been less than 110 percent of quota and as much as 150 percent of quota.

SALES MANAGEMENT

Q. What is the hardest part of being a sales manager?

The first thing is to be able to choose really good, motivated people. Then teach them the process of successful sales, monitor the process, and hold them accountable.

SOFTWARE ENGINEER

Q. What are your strengths as a software engineer?

I'm a fast, head-down coder who writes unbreakable, bulletproof code. I require minimal supervision, get along really well with everybody, and will meld beautifully with your team.

SOLUTION ARCHITECT

Q. What have been your biggest professional challenges?

The obstacles I face include the fact that we have many departments using systems that aren't connected, leading to data duplication and sometimes multiple versions of the "truth." It's not enough to keep machines and applications running; I have to make sure that critical information can move through these systems and reach the right people at the right time.

9 Powerful Phrases for Clarifying the Job Offer and Discussing Money

One of the biggest challenges you have in your job search is to manage unemotionally, objectively, and mindfully the process of finding a job from one step to the next step. Most people get to the "finals" and quit working the process. They think that when they reach third base, it's just a matter of time before they reach home. This is a big mistake! You cannot afford to count on anything until you actually have an offer and a start date.

Almost everything about a job opportunity can change between the initial search for a candidate and the final offer and acceptance. If there's anything I've learned since 1973, it's that what companies normally start out looking for in an employee from the top to the bottom of the organization—the titles they will give, the duties and responsibilities that are associated with a particular job, and, probably most important, the money they're willing to pay for it—can change anywhere from a small amount to a drastic amount from the beginning of the job search to the filling of the position.

I've experienced candidates getting starting salaries as much as $60,000 a year more than what a company originally wanted to pay. They accomplished this simply because they did not qualify themselves out of the opportunity in the initial part of the interviewing process, and they proved value to warrant a larger starting salary. Too often, candidates start qualifying opportunities before they establish their value to a prospective employer.

Continue to sell yourself and communicate what you can do for a company right up to the point that you are the one the organization wants to hire. Then you can talk about what the company can do for you.

QUESTIONS TO ASK AT THE TIME OF AN OFFER

Before accepting any job offer, you must ask yourself: "Do I clearly understand everything I need know about this job?"

Up until now, your interviewing process has pretty much been a one-way street. If you've sold yourself like you should have, the hiring authority wants to answer all of the questions you may have. He or she wants a win-win deal, too. Once you are told that you're the person a company would like to hire and they want to make you an offer, it is your turn to start asking questions. Explain that you would like to have a meeting with the hiring authority and get as much clarification about all the questions you might have about the job offer. Unless the hiring authority is out of state, always have this kind of discussion face-to-face. Never do this over the phone, unless you absolutely have to.

When you meet with the hiring authority, he or she may think that you're ready to accept the job, or at least start talking about specifics such as title, money, and so on. You should start out using the following phrase:

Mr. or Ms. _____, I'm really excited about this opportunity. However, I have a number of questions about things that I would like to discuss with you. So, before we get down to the nitty-gritty, I'd like to find out . . .

Prepare a list of questions about the opportunity that you are either unclear about or haven't had a chance to ask before. The hiring authority will have covered or explained many of the issues that you might ask about in the interviewing process. However, now is the time to get clarification. Do not hesitate to get into as much detail as you need in your analysis of the offer. And do not hesitate to ask for an audience with anyone whom you feel can answer your questions. As much as you can, make sure you have a clear understanding of everything before you consider accepting the job.

There should be no loose ends or unanswered questions. Sit down and write out everything you think you know about the job that you gathered in the interviewing process. Write down all the questions that are not clear to you. Then ask your questions using the phrases that follow in this chapter and take notes on the answers.

Q. What are your professional and personal expectations of me?

If you don't already know, you certainly want and need to know the answer at this point. Don't be surprised if you hear some aspects of the job that you don't recall hearing before. Often, in the interviewing process, assumptions by both parties are made. You've been focused on selling yourself, but you now want to be sure you totally understand the expectations.

Q. Can you describe the working environment here?

The interviewing process probably gave you a really good feel for this, but you want to hear it. Pay special attention to the metaphors and analogies you will hear.

Q. What is your management style?

On average, you've probably only spent one or two hours with this person in a rather contrived atmosphere. You want to listen to make sure what you hear is consistent with what you saw or experienced. Again, listen to the metaphors.

Q. What is the management style of your boss and the company?

If you hear, "Well, my boss is totally different than me. He's a real piece of work," or, "This company is pretty tyrannical, but we operate differently in this group," you'll get one impression. If you hear, "It's pretty consistent with my style," you'll get another impression. You just need to know.

Q. What are your personal plans with the company?

By throwing in some personal questions now and then, you create a conversational environment, rather than an interview environment. "We are all in this together" becomes more real when you ask about the hiring authority's personal future.

Q. How would you describe the philosophy of the company as well as your personal philosophy?

You may have already gotten a picture of both of these in the interviewing process, but it doesn't hurt to ask again to see if you get consistency. You don't have to agree with everyone's philosophy, but you do have to feel compatible with it

Q. How would you describe the culture and values of the company?

Culture can be a tricky issue. If you hear, "Well, we work hard, but we also party hard," and you are not that kind of person, you may not fit in. If you hear, "We are here for the money, and that is all we care about," and you're passionate about personal growth and not concerned about money, you might want to dig deeper to see if you can live with this approach. If you are young and single and expect a social life with your co-workers and you hear, "We are very family oriented here. Most of us are grandparents. We work hard, but don't socialize with each other outside of work," this job may not be a source of social relationships.

Q. How would you describe my potential peers?

It is good to get an idea of what the boss thinks of all of the people you will be working with. Listen to the metaphors and analogies. If your potential bosses describe your potential peers as "slugs," "lazy," "less than competent," or "brilliant," "wonderful," "great," they will probably say the same thing about you someday soon if you take the job.

Q. If I were to accept this offer, what can I do when I start to be most effective and contribute to alleviating your biggest problem?

Potential employers love to hear this kind of question. It shows that you really are concerned about what you can do for them. Therefore, when you are considering an offer, that is, what they might be able to do for you, you're showing concern about what you can do for them. In other words, keep selling!

Q. What is the percentage of turnover in the company?

Don't be surprised if your hiring authority doesn't really know the answer to this question. The only time your hiring authority is going to know this is if turnover in the company is very high. If you find out that turnover is high by asking this question, the hiring authority will automatically explain to you why. The reason may make a big difference as to whether or not you take the job.

Q. What is the turnover in this department?

Again, you certainly want to find this out. If there is a great deal of turnover in the department, the hiring authority will automatically give you the reasons why. The answer to this question may or may not make a difference in your taking the job. However, you at least need to know what you're getting into.

Q. How often is there turnover in the job I'm discussing with you?

You may already know this from the interviewing process, but you might want to confirm it. If it seems higher than normal, it is fair to ask "Why?" If the answer is, "We promote out of this position often," it is one thing. If it is, "We can't find anyone to do the job right," you may want to ask more questions.

Q. What are the major problems facing the company and this department?

Notice if this is consistent with what you have heard before. Often, in the final stages of the interviewing process, a hiring authority may come clean with you about issues in the company or the department that no one wanted to mention before. Up until now they didn't want to discourage you as a candidate, but now they don't want you to be shocked at some issue the first day you show up for the job.

Q. What are the traits you see in me that are good for this job and made you want to hire me?

You need to know how you are perceived by the hiring authority.

Q. Based on what you know of me, what might my weaknesses be in light of this job?

Again, you just want to know what the expectations are. The perception of you and how you really are once you are on the job will be different. Don't worry about the weaknesses; we all have them. Again, you want to get an idea of expectations.

Q. Why do you want to hire me? What did I demonstrate to you that the other candidates didn't?

Listen closely to this answer. You might have assumed certain reasons why you're being offered the job. You will also learn what you did to outdistance the other candidates. This information may come in handy if you need to negotiate regarding salary and benefits when the time is right.

Q. Why didn't you hire from within?

You probably already know the answer, but it doesn't hurt to ask again, now that things are getting serious. Don't be surprised if you hear, "We sure came close to promoting from within and if we don't work things out with you, that is what we might do." A little leverage just slipped away.

Q. What aspects of the job or the company am I going to be surprised about?

The hiring authorities probably will think a minute and then either drop a bombshell on you with a fact or some information that will shock you, or they will say something neutral like, "What a nice person I am."

Q. What are the worst aspects of the job?

These issues may have been mentioned somewhere in the interviewing process, but now that things are getting serious you need to make sure you know them.

Q. Is the company planning any layoffs or downsizings?

This will be a simple "no" or "not that I know of," or "oh, yeah, we go through that every year or so." When you get this last answer, be bold and ask, "If there are layoffs, how will it affect this job?" It is obvious that no one is going to intentionally go to the trouble of hiring anyone and then lay them off soon after they hire them. But I have seen candidates who were hired and within a month or so laid off. No one can predict these things . . . or at least will never admit to it.

Q. How will my success be measured in this job?

You need to know exactly how your success will be measured. If you are in sales, it is obvious that you will be measured by the sales you make and the quota you attain. But success in other professional positions is not quite as easy to measure. Also find out if and how this measurement will be reflected in salary reviews. Get specifics and write them down. You don't want to take a job and later be surprised by the way performance and salary reviews are practiced.

Q. How is performance measured? How often? How does that relate to the job I'm considering?

You may be shocked to find that many firms have no formal performance measurement systems. If there is a formal performance measurement procedure, you'll now find out what it is. Pay particular attention to find out if salary reviews or incentive bonuses are associated with the tools the company uses. Don't fret if a company doesn't have a formal performance measurement program; just know what they do use. Get copies of the procedure or performance measurement tools if you can.

Q. What happened to the last person in the job?

You need to know this. If the person was fired, you need to know the circumstances. If you learned the answer to this question during the interviewing process, you will want to get clarification now. I have known candidates to track down the person who was fired to get an idea about the situation. If a person was promoted out of the job, ask to speak to that person. You want to learn as much as you can about what you are getting into and this is a great way to do it.

Q. Is the company seeking to grow? How?

Very few organizations are going to tell you that they don't want to grow. But, if you have done your homework, you will know what the track record of growth, or lack of it, has been for the company itself. You've probably also picked up the direction that the company is going during the interviewing process. Some organizations will admit that they don't want to grow too rapidly. If a company intends to grow by acquisition or merger, it may affect your particular position. Acquiring a company or a merger can create function duplication. If they are in the process of being sold, you need to know that, too.

A standard follow-up question here, no matter what you're told should be:

Q. So, how might that affect this position?

Listen carefully to the answer. Most of the time, you're going to hear something like, "Oh, it really won't matter!" You'd better listen to how the person says this more than what they say. Often, companies need to hire somebody because they need a certain task or job done immediately. They may or may not be thinking, or even care, about what might happen to the position in the future. Growth, or lack of it, may not affect the job you're interviewing for one way or the other. Simply listen to the answer, and then follow your gut.

Q. Exactly how much travel is involved with the job?

Usually, if there is an inordinate amount of travel involved in a job, you would have heard about it during the interviewing process. However, if there is travel involved in a particular job, you need to know exactly how much. So, get a very specific number of days and number of nights per week or per month that travel is required. One person's definition of "some travel" is different than another person's. You need to know in terms relative to what you can or can't do.

Q. Is there relocation now or down the road?

If immediate relocation is involved in the position, you will probably learn about it in the initial part of the interviewing process. Relocation is an expensive venture and companies don't do it unless there's real value for them. It is often cheaper to find someone in the local area to do a specific job than it is to relocate someone, even a proven employee, to where the job is. If relocation is involved now or later, be sure that you are clear about what the company will and won't do regarding relocation.

Q. How long do you plan to be in your position with the company?

How someone answers this is as important as what they say. Once in a while, a hiring authority will tell you how long they plan to stay in the job. It is good to know if the hiring authority has plans beyond his or her present position. If you get an answer like, "Most people here stay in their positions for about three years and then rotate to other departments of the organization," you'll realize that you will be faced with the same opportunity. If you get, ""I have absolutely no idea. I just take things day-to-day, month-to-month, and year-to-year," then at least you have an idea of how this person feels about his or her future.

Q. Why have people in the past failed to do well at this job?

This is a great question. Often, you will have gotten a sense of how people did in the job you're interviewing for before you get to this point. However, it's a really good idea to ask this question at the time of getting an offer. If you hadn't gotten the real reason as to why people have failed before, you will probably get it now. The reason you hear can be very revealing and may end up making a difference in your taking the job. Listen very carefully to the answer that you get to this question. Whatever the hiring authority tells you, they may be saying this same thing about you some day.

Q. What are the company's major strengths and weaknesses?

Now that the company is strongly considering you and they're trying to hire you, you might hear more than just the party line. Don't necessarily expect something different than you've already heard, but it doesn't hurt to ask. Since you're now being invited to be an insider in the company, you may get a more realistic idea about strengths and weaknesses.

Q. What are your personal strengths and weaknesses?

The best time to ask this question is right after you ask the same question about the company. You asked a similar question when you asked this person what it was like to work for them. Let this person talk about their personal strengths and weaknesses. Listen carefully to what they say. The kind of strengths and weaknesses this person describes will be the kind of things he will look for in others, that is, you! Take good notes. See if what you hear is consistent with what your potential peers say about this person.

Q. Can you explain the organizational structure of the company and of the department?

This is pretty simple and straightforward. You may have been unable to find this out before this interview.

Q. What are the trends in your industry?

If you've done your research correctly, you will know the answers to this already. But it doesn't hurt to find out what your potential boss thinks.

Q. Does the company have any present or pending legal issues?

You'll probably be one of the few, if not the only, candidates who asks this question. If you've done your homework, you already know most of the legal entanglements that the company may be involved in. This is not only asking about those but also any pending ones. It's rare for businesses not to be involved in some minor litigation, but major litigation can literally put small businesses in great jeopardy. If the hiring authority does not mention a legal issue that you know could have some major impact on the company—and therefore your new job if you accept it—now is the time to ask about it. Be sure you understand where the litigation might be before you accept a job.

Q. How is the department perceived by the rest of the company?

Notice the metaphors that the person uses to describe how the department is perceived. Whatever description the hiring authority uses is likely the way he thinks he is perceived. So, if he says something like, "We are very respected because we provide accurate information on time," or, "The performance of the department affects everybody in the company, so we're very careful," you probably know what you're getting into. Likewise, if the person says, "We are the most hated department in the company because we say 'no' to everything and everybody," you'll have a different impression.

Q. Are there written goals for the department? Who sets them?

Even if there are not formal goals for the department, this is a good question to ask. If the department has formal goals for the year, it would be a good idea to ask to see them. If the goals are imposed on the department, you'll find that out. If the department does not have any written goals, you'll find that out, too. The sales department with no written or formal goals cannot be very effective. The accounting or purchasing department may be a different story.

Q. How many people have been in the job in the last five years? Where are they now?

Listen carefully to this answer. If no one that had been in this job in the last five years is still with the company, it may not be a good thing. If people are promoted regularly out of this position, that may be good. If there is a high degree of turnover in this job, you need to know why. If you hear, "Everyone who has been in this position has been incompetent," watch out! No matter how good you think you are, the same thing may be said about you in the future. If you hear, "Well, I really don't know why people leave this job so often," you need to do further investigation. See the next question.

Q. May I speak with the person that has left (or is leaving) the job?

If the person presently in the job or the person that's leaving the job is still with the company, you should be given access to them with no problem. If you can't speak to the person who is presently in the job or has been at the position most recently, you will not get a tremendous insight into the job. In some instances, the company may not want you to get exposure to the person who is presently in the job. This shouldn't be a deal killer one way or the other. Listen carefully to the circumstances that have caused the position to be open.

Q. What would be my access to you? Daily, weekly, monthly?

You'll get a really good idea of the manager's style when he or she answers this question. You will also get a sense of how much autonomy you may have in the job. Balance the answer to this question with the answer you get to how much authority you might have. If you have a lot of responsibility but very little authority, and you only see or hear from your boss once a month, you may be in for a real challenge.

QUESTIONS TO ASK WHEN THE POSITION INVOLVES MANAGEMENT

What follows are questions for this specific scenario with further explanations.

Q. Why are there no internal candidates for this job?

This is the biggest question that you need answered. Companies have a tendency to promote from within, so if you're interviewing for a management position, you better get a very clear and convincing set of reasons as to why no one has been promoted from within. There may be some very legitimate, reasonable business reasons as to why there are no internal candidates capable of being promoted. But it also might be that nobody in the company wanted the job! Even though you may want the job and it may very well be good for you, you must be absolutely comfortable with the answer to this question.

Q. How much authority will I have in running the department (the group, the facility, and so on)?

You already may have picked up on a lot of the authority you will have in the interviewing process. But, now you need to get a real, detailed understanding of your authority. Having profit and loss responsibility usually carries a lot more authority than not having it. Don't assume you'll have it because you think you heard it in the interviewing process. You were focused on selling yourself then; now you are focused on qualifying the job, your expectations, your ability to do it, and your desire to land.

Q. I would like to speak to peers about the position that I am interviewing for. Can we arrange that?

Unless the organization you're interviewing with is replacing somebody confidentially, it should allow you to talk to managers in the same kind of position you are applying for. You'll get more insights about the company and the job from your potential peers, and especially those in management positions, than you will from anyone else in the company, even the people you were interviewing with. If the organization doesn't want you to talk to other managers, it should raise a big red flag to you. Even if filling the position is confidential and they're replacing someone without their knowledge, a hiring authority should be able to provide you with other managers who may talk to you on a confidential basis. Don't underestimate what you'll learn by doing this.

Q. Are there any difficult personalities on the staff that I will be supervising?

Pay attention to the hiring authorities' initial response to your question. If he or she hesitates and has to answer the question carefully or pensively, you know that you might have real challenges here. Let the hiring authority describe to you all of the people on the staff that he knows about. People are often really uncomfortable when they get a new supervisor. So you need to be prepared for any difficulties, especially difficult personalities that you may inherit.

Q. Are there any members of the staff that should be let go?

Many times when a new manager is being brought on board, people who ought to be fired or moved around are left in their place until the new manager is hired. Upper management will insist that there is enough turmoil going on with hiring a new manager and simply leave the difficult task to the new hire. Be ready for any kind of answer to this question. If there are really big problems, you will probably have heard about them during the interviewing process. But now it is time to press on this. Unless you are very lucky, you will probably have to replace one or more of the staff members. You can assume these people should have been let go a long time ago, and their dismissal has been postponed because it is enough of a hassle to find a new manager. So, listen well.

Q. How are the people in the department going to react to an outsider as a manager?

You may have gotten a hint of this answer in the interviewing process. However, the hiring authority that you were talking to is so interested in the moment, that is, getting someone hired for the position, they don't really care what reaction a new manager is going to get. Trust me, if you are in this situation, there's enough emotion throughout the whole staff that it is going to take a number of months for everything to settle down. No matter what you're told in answering this question, assume the worst.

Q. May I speak with the staff I will be managing?

Unless the present person is being replaced or the hiring is strictly confidential, you should be allowed to talk to all of the people that you're going to be managing. You will have a much better understanding of what you're walking into after you do this. I would recommend you begin with the administrative or support staff. These people always have a very clear idea of what's going on in a department, both positive and negative. Should you take the job, you're going to hear it anyhow, so you might as well start now. If you're not allowed to talk to the staff that you might be supervising, take that as a big red flag.

Q. What are the biggest problems in the department?

The answer to this question will be interesting. If you're told the same things that you heard from the staff you were going to supervise, then you're in real good shape. At least everybody knows what the problems are. If there were no problems that needed to be solved, they wouldn't need to hire you or anybody else to solve them. The key here is to find out if everyone from upper management on down agrees with what the problems are. Even if they don't agree, at least you will know what everyone's point of view is.

Q. What condition is morale in and why?

This can be part of the previous question. After you've spoken to all the people you will be supervising, you will know how morale is. The reason you ask this question of upper management is to find out if what they feel and what the subordinates that will be working for you feel are the same. Don't be surprised if they're not.

Q. Who are the problem employees?

You're probably going to find this out when you interview everybody on the potential new staff. But it is always better to get upper management's opinion. If you are forewarned about who is going to be your biggest challenge, you might approach them a little differently. Don't be surprised if you're told that no one is a real problem, but you find out the contrary once you interview the potential staff.

Q. Who are the stars that can help my transition go smoothly?

Like with the previous question, forewarned is forearmed. You'll get a great idea about who can help you and who can hinder you if you interview everyone in the correct way. But it doesn't hurt to have upper management's ideas about who will support you the best.

Q. Are there any staff members that are in line for a promotion? Did any of them apply for this job?

The first part of this question is asked in order to get an answer to the second part. It's nice to know whom upper management thinks might be good to promote. But it is imperative that you know who among your potential new staff has applied for the job that you are considering. If you wind up supervising someone who applied for the job that you accept, their not getting the job may have a real impact on your relationship with them. These people can be extremely helpful in your transition as a new manager, if they want to be. They can also be your worst nightmare and sabotage just about everything you'd do. Supervising a person who thought that they were qualified to do the job you got takes a lot of careful communication and interaction.

Q. If I have budgetary responsibility, how large is the budget? Has the department been above or below budget, presently and in the recent past?

You need to know what kind of an economic situation you might be walking into. Hiring authorities may not want to offer this information. In recent economic times, budgets have been slashed and yet performance expectations have been high. If your two predecessors have left or moved on because they couldn't get their job done with the budget they have been given, you need to know. If the department or group has gone over budget, you need to ask the obvious, "Why?"

Q. What kind of reports am I going to be responsible for? Are they internal company reports, or governmental ones?

In these days of Sarbanes-Oxley laws, public companies especially, but private ones, too, are much more careful about most everything financial. Departments such as sales, which traditionally didn't have to be much concerned about reporting, now have to be very careful about how they report sales the company has made. They can no longer easily report sales that make things look good for a while, then go back and amend the reports later. If you've been in financial positions, you are probably familiar with all of the kinds of governmental reports you will be responsible for. But it certainly doesn't hurt to make sure you have a clear idea about what you will be responsible for and what you won't.

Q. Does the company plan to make any immediate acquisitions or be acquired or change in any way that might affect the job we are discussing?

Look for hesitancy on the part of the hiring authority when answering this question. If you do find out that the company is up for sale or looking to be acquired, think about the kind of position that you're interviewing for and what kind of duplicity there might be in another organization. If you sense that there may be an issue here, it certainly doesn't hurt to just bluntly ask the hiring authority something like, "Look, I really don't want to accept a position and then be involved in a merger or acquisition and have the job I take be at risk. Is there a chance of that happening?" If the hiring authority has any integrity at all and there is some kind of pending event, he or she will tell you.

Q. What is the greatest opportunity facing the company? Its greatest challenge?

Asking this question allows the hiring authority to give a balanced answer. The "greatest opportunity" might be nice to know, but your real interest is in finding out what the "greatest challenge" is. If the greatest challenge is surviving a gigantic lawsuit, you need to know. The answer to this question will most often be fairly benign, but you just might be surprised at any answer you might get. It might be one that could change your whole opinion of the opportunity. *Caveat emptor.*

DISCUSSING MONEY

The hiring authority will usually have questions for you to answer regarding money. Most people think that these are some of the most difficult questions to deal with in the interviewing process. Frankly, if all of the other questions about being able to do the job, being liked, and being a risk are answered, even reasonably well, these questions about money are relatively easy to deal with. In fact, the answers to these questions are merely an outgrowth of all of the previous ones. The more an organization wants to hire you and the more you want to go to work for them, the easier it is to work out the money. So, the better you sell yourself and the more desirable you are to an organization, the more likely they are to compensate you fairly.

Q. What are you currently earning? or What have you been earning most recently? (This is a simple question and requires a simple answer. Just share with the hiring authority exactly what you have been earning or are presently earning. Whatever you do, don't inflate the numbers.)

In my present (past) position I'm earning $_____.

Q. What kind of money would you like to earn? (Hopefully, you will have some idea about the salary range for the position that you are interviewing for. However, your stock answer in a situation like this should be the following.)

I'd like to earn as much as I can, commensurate with the service that I give. I am just as interested in a fulfilling and challenging position as I am in the money I want to earn. I have found that if the position is right for me, and I am right for the company that I'm going to go work for, the money is usually going to take care of itself. What kind of money for this position did your organization have in mind?

Always discuss money in relationship to the job that needs to be done.

Q. What kind of salary (or earnings) are you looking for? (This is a slightly different version of the previous question.)

Salary and earnings are important, but equally as important to me is the company, the job, the people, and the future. In the past (or presently), *I have been earning $_____. What is the salary* (or earnings) *associated with this job?*

Q. You have been making $_____ and the money associated with this position is significantly less. How do we know that you will be happy? (In this situation, you have to find out exactly how much of a difference there is between what you have been making and what this particular position pays. If you have been out of work for any amount of time, the truth is at this point you are making absolutely nothing.)

I realize there is a difference between what I have made (. . . . or what I am making now) and this position. However, I have found that if the opportunity is right and I am able to perform at my best, the difference in the money isn't as important as the quality of the job and the opportunity.

Q. What is the most money that you have ever made? (Answer this question judiciously. If you've been in sales, for instance, and your earnings have fluctuated over the years, give an average of the last few years. Bragging about making a lot of money will never help in negotiations. If you made an inordinate amount of money several years ago, I would recommend not even mentioning it. Again, the answer to a question like this has to center around not just what you've earned, but the challenge of the job opportunity itself.)

There have been a few years in which I've been fortunate enough to be with organizations where my bonus earnings were sizable. But I realize that those are very uncommon. I am more interested in the opportunity, the challenge of the job, and the potential. If those things are taken care of, my earnings will reflect my performance.

Q. What do you consider most important: a high salary, job recognition, or advancement? (Once again, combining earnings with job performance is the best thing you can do.)

I have found that the better job I do and the harder I work, recognition, advancement, and, especially, money usually take care of themselves.

Q. What kind of benefits are you expecting? (In the past few years, benefit plans, especially in the insurance area, have sky-rocketed in costs, particularly for companies with a hundred people or less. So, there is no such thing as "standard" benefits. It is not uncommon for organizations to have drastically reduced their benefit plans for their employees. The purpose of this question is to find out if there is going to be a great deal of difference between the kind of benefits that you have had before and the kind of benefits that might be offered with this company. Again, you really don't want concerns about benefits to interrupt the interviewing process until you have finally sold yourself.)

Benefits, like money, to me are not as important as the company, the job, and the professional challenge. I will certainly take the benefits package into consideration if an offer is made, but right now those kinds of things shouldn't be an issue.

Some candidates jump the gun and start negotiating money before they hear the whole offer. It's not a good idea to pick out one or two issues about an offer until you have heard and completely understand all of the compensation, benefits program, and any other aspects of the offer. Things like base salary, salary reviews, commissions, and so forth may have a great flexibility. After you've heard the entire offer and you want to negotiate the salary, here is the most successful way to do it:

Remember, Mr. or Ms. _____, I do want this job. My employment here will be good for both of us. However, I need to ask, is that the best you can do regarding the salary?

Then stop talking! If the hiring authority responds with something like, "Why do you ask?," you'd better have a good reason, such as:

Well, my last salary was (is) $60,000, and I'd like to see if we can get to $65,000. What can we do to get there?

Now is the time to negotiate. If you've managed the interviewing process correctly, you already have a good idea of what the salary and compensation range for the position is. Money is simply a part of the job offer negotiation. Treat money with grace and ease, like any other part of the interviewing process.

INDEX